❧ Endorsement ❧

I love how Wendy helps us dig into Scripture so we can truly and personally grasp the deep love God has for us. This is an amazingly solid study that will get you excited to study the Bible and breathe fresh life into your heart.

—**Lysa TerKeurst**, *New York Times* bestselling author and president of Proverbs 31 Ministries

1 John

I Am Loved

WENDY BLIGHT

HarperChristian
Resources

1 John
© 2017 by Wendy Blight

Requests for information should be addressed to:
HarperChristian Resources, 3900 Sparks Dr. SE, Grand Rapids, Michigan 49546

Previously published as *I Am Loved* by Wendy Blight (2017).

ISBN 978-0-310-14118-1 (softcover)
ISBN 978-0-310-14119-8 (ebook)

Page design and layout: CrosslinCreative.net

Published in association with the literary agency of Wolgemuth & Associates, Inc.

Any Internet addresses (websites, blogs, etc.) and telephone numbers in this book are offered as a resource. They are not intended in any way to be or imply an endorsement by HarperChristian Resources, nor does HarperChristian Resources vouch for the content of these sites and numbers for the life of this study guide.

HarperChristian Resources titles may be purchased in bulk for church, business, fundraising, or ministry use. For information, please e-mail ResourceSpecialist@ ChurchSource.com.

First Printing July 2021 / Printed in the United States of America

Dedication

I DEDICATE THIS BOOK to Bobbie Wolgemuth, my dear friend and spiritual mom, who has now passed through the heavens to be with the One she adored. Bobbie lived loved and modeled in the most excellent way how to make expressions of that love the pattern of her life. We were beneficiaries of that love. She poured godly wisdom, countless prayers, and God's living and active Word into my mama's heart in ways that transformed my heart, my marriage, and my home. Bobbie's love has left a legacy that has had, and will continue to have, ripple effects on women, families, and generations to come.

⇛ *Acknowledgments* ⇚

THE MORE I WRITE, the more I appreciate the friends and family God has placed around me on this amazing journey called life.

Monty—From the day I married you, you've modeled the unconditional love and acceptance of the Father. You make every day fun, and I can't wait to live out the rest of my days with you!

Lauren and Bo—God's precious gifts to me. You've left our nest but not our hearts. I pray you've taken with you the assurance of God's deep and abiding love and the power of that love to transform your lives. And, thanks for letting me share your stories!

Aunt Sal and Aunt Peggy—Thank you for your prayers, love, and words of encouragement. I love you both, and it's been a joy to watch God's Word and His work come alive in your lives.

Lisa Sheltra—my dearest friend and editor extraordinaire. You make me a better writer with each and every book. Your love and encouragement as friend and editor means more than you'll ever know.

Proverbs 31 On-Line Bible Study Team—I treasure each one of you. The impact of your friendship and support in my life and ministry is immeasurable. I love partnering with you to engage women with God's living and active Word in a fresh way through Bible study and community.

Erik Wolgemuth—I'm grateful for your wisdom and direction as I continue on this journey of writing and teaching God's Word.

HarperCollins Christian Publishing Team—It's a joy and privilege to partner with you again to encourage and equip women to dig deeper into God's living and active Word.

❧ Contents ❧

❧ Message from My Heart ❧

I WROTE THIS MESSAGE FOR EVERY WOMAN who craves to truly understand, walk confidently in, and live out God's unconditional, extravagant, lavish love. It's a love I didn't understand, let alone live, until I exposed my heart to the words John penned in this letter. Because let's be real. It's hard to love like God does. It's hard to love a parent who abandoned us as a child. It's hard to love a girlfriend who betrayed us. It's hard to love a God who doesn't heal debilitating, chronic pain.

But God destined us for this kind of love. To know it personally. To walk in it confidently. And most especially, to live it for all to see. Spending months and months with John and his words allowed God to lovingly transform my heart in ways I could not have imagined. As I write these words, I am praying the same for you. In fact, from the very first day I sat down to write this study, I prayed for every woman who would one day hold this book in her hand. And because *you* now hold this book in *your* hand, you have been prayed for, my friend! So, although we haven't met personally, God has already connected our hearts in the heavenly places. By His Spirit, He has knit our hearts together for this moment in time as we open His Word together.

You'll find John's words highly relevant because he wrote to an audience living in a culture not unlike our own. Through his unique perspective as Jesus's last living disciple, John sets forth what it looks like to love and live authentically for Christ.

At times, John's words will be tender and encouraging. But at other times, they will be quite challenging as he warns against false teachers, instructs us how to identify and confront them, and exhorts us to live lives of obedience.

Because we'll invest much of our heart and time in the words of this disciple, we should get to know him better. I always pictured John as gentle and tenderhearted. Reserved and introspective. As I came to know him through his writings, I discovered another side of this man of God. One far different from the John I just described.

I found him to be bold, direct, even demanding at times. A man who had a strong presence among the disciples. A leader. Absolute in his thinking.

But one thing is certain. Whether reading the words penned by the younger, brasher John or the older, wiser John, his words are trustworthy. They are the words of a man who walked with Jesus. Spoke with Jesus. Prayed with Jesus. Did life with Jesus. A man who gazed into Jesus's eyes. Heard His voice. Held His hands. Felt His heartbeat.

John's words also stand the test of time. He unabashedly proclaims truth . . . always. But he proclaims it in love and with love . . . always. Our world needs this balance today because love spoken without truth is hollow and empty. It carries no weight. Truth spoken without love is legalism and rules. It leads to condemnation.

Over the years, John's time with Jesus transformed his heart. Jesus softened it and reined it in. He shifted John's teaching methods to master the task of speaking the hard truths with great love.

More than any other New Testament writer, John wrote about love. Here is a sampling of His words on love:

♥ God is a God of love.

♥ God is love.

♥ God loved the world.

♥ God loved His Son.

♥ Jesus loved the disciples.

♥ Jesus loves us.

♥ We are called to love one another.

That's a lot of love, ya'll!

Yet, John made clear God's love is a love that is never compromised. It never tolerates deception, lies, or any type of sin. So, at times, you might find John's words harsh. You might even strongly disagree with him. When you find yourself in that place, remember John's heart. John teaches truth in no uncertain terms. But those truths are bathed in and delivered from a heart of love.

Friend, I'm sure you would agree, now more than ever our world desperately needs to hear, know, and understand God's truth spoken in love. Let it begin here. With us. Today.

INTRODUCTION

*I*f you are doing this study with a group, use these questions as a guide for your group discussion before you dig into the first week of study!

1. I love new beginnings. The start of a new Bible study is a great new beginning. Opening God's Word with fresh eyes and asking Him to speak personally to me brings greater anticipation to my study time. What are you asking God to do in your life as you begin your journey through the pages of 1 John?

   _____

   _____

2. Each week of the study begins with a prayer written from my heart to yours. I encourage you to write your own prayer as you begin this study. Using your answer to Question 1, take a few minutes to write a prayer. Invite God to meet you each time you open His Word, and invite His Holy Spirit to give you a spirit of wisdom and understanding and to teach you how to practically apply what you are learning to your everyday life.

   _____

   _____

   _____

_____

_____

_____

3. As we begin this book written by John, the disciple Jesus loved, share facts you know and any thoughts you have about him.

_____

_____

_____

4. God's Word fills nearly every page of this study. Not a day will pass that you won't meet God in His living and active Word. That Word brings with it unsearchable riches and treasures. Look up the following truths, promises, and commands, asking God to bring them alive in your heart as you meet Him each day.

   a. Deuteronomy 6:6–9

   b. Deuteronomy 8:3

   c. Psalm 119:130

   d. Jeremiah 15:16

   e. Isaiah 55:11

   f. Hebrews 4:12

   g. James 1:22

WEEK

ONE

WALK IN THE LIGHT

PRAYER: *Oh God, I'm excited for a new journey through Your Word. Open my eyes to see, my ears to hear, and my heart to understand eternal mysteries that only You can reveal on this exciting adventure through the book of Your "beloved," John. Carve out time for me each day to spend with You. Give me the discipline to do my work, the perseverance to continue when I want to give up, and the mind to practically apply all that I learn. Reveal marvelous new truths and promises from Your Word. Draw me close. Speak into my life and transform my heart and mind in fresh new ways. I ask all this in Jesus's name, Amen.*

Meet John

MEMORY VERSE: *This is the message we have heard from him and declare to you: God is light; in him there is no darkness at all.* (1 John 1:5)

*D*o you remember the first time your parents left you alone? I do. I don't have many vivid childhood memories, but this night I remember. Our neighbors had invited my parents to a dinner party. They gave me fair warning and encouraged me to "be a big girl" and stay home by myself. The very thought terrified me. I wanted to jump up and down, stomp my feet and scream, "No!" But I didn't.

The dreaded night finally arrived. Orange and purple hues adorned the sky as the sun began to slip behind the horizon. Heart pounding, I watched my parents walk out the door, down the sidewalk, and into the fading light.

This won't be so bad.

I shut and locked the door. I was alone. All alone.

My stomach twisted and turned as darkness consumed the sky. I remembered my Dad's last words, delivered through kind eyes, "Don't forget. We're just a phone call away."

But I wouldn't call. I couldn't call. I needed to do this.

In the quietness, I walked over to the television and turned it on. Yes, in those days you had to actually walk over to the television to turn it on! I'm giving away my age here. I then hopped onto the couch, grabbed a pillow, and curled up with my favorite blanket. My selection for the night, *The Carol Burnett Show*. What better way to take my mind off my fears?

But my stomach continued to churn.

Familiar furniture, plants, and bushes took on strange shapes and sizes. I imagined bad guys lurking inside and out. Crouching . . . watching . . . waiting for me to go to bed.

Why did they have to leave me tonight? I'm not old enough. I don't want to be alone.

Bedtime arrived and that meant walking through the scary shadows.

Why didn't I close the blinds? Why didn't I turn those lights on before it got dark?

Tears spilled down my cheeks. *I hate this.* Clutching my blanket, I tip-toed through the dining room. *If I could just reach the light switch.* It seemed miles away. *What if someone's watching?* Again, I envisioned the scary man waiting . . . watching me outside the window.

The imagined terrified me.

I wanted my parents.

Finally, I reached the light switch, flipped it up, and light flooded every dark space. Everything looked familiar again. I felt safe.

The real replaced my imagined. The imagined fears that held the little girl in my story captive dissipated the moment light flooded the room.

It's a simple fact, my friend. Light dispels darkness. With light, there are no more illusions . . . no more imagined fears. Light brings clarity, safety, and security.

My little-girl fears perfectly illustrate a scriptural nugget tucked in the first chapter of John's letter.

But, before going any further, let's get to know the author of 1 John, the man with whom we will become intimately acquainted over the next five weeks. His name is John. He often called himself "the disciple whom Jesus loved" (John 13:23).

We first meet John in Matthew 4:21. Not long after Jesus called His first two disciples, Peter and Andrew, He encountered two brothers named James and John (also called the sons of Zebedee). Like Peter and Andrew, they were fishermen. Simple, hardworking men going about their business. Jesus called them by name while they were with their father getting ready to cast out their nets for the day. Upon hearing Jesus's call, they did not ask questions or give excuses. Scripture says, "[I]mmediately they left the boat and their father and followed him" (Matthew 4:22).

Wow! Immediate obedience. Wish I could say I always react that way when Jesus calls out to me. All too often, I don't.

James and John left family and all that was familiar to follow this man they barely knew. For the next three years, John and eleven other disciples walked alongside Jesus, watching Him turn water into wine, heal the sick, feed thousands with nothing but a few loaves and fish, and—most amazingly—bring the dead back to life.

Read and record what the following passages reveal about John.

♥ Luke 9:51–56

_____

_____

♥ Mark 9:33–37

_____

_____

♥ Matthew 20:20–28 (What do these verses communicate about John's relationship with his mother?)

_____

_____

7

♥ **What was Jesus's response to her request?**

_____

_____

I can so relate to John because I am quick to take offense. Quick to lose my temper. What about you? And don't we all at one time or another long to hold that place of honor in someone's heart or at their table?

Those were John's younger days. An amazing transformation occurred between the time Jesus found him fishing and the time he wrote this letter. In 1 John, we see a different man. A gentler man. A kinder man. A man motivated by deep love for God and for God's people.

John matured over the years as he walked alongside Jesus, observed His ways, experienced His love, listened to His teachings, and obeyed the call to full-time ministry.

My favorite image of John comes near the end of Jesus's life as He gathered His disciples around a table to share a message and meal. Scripture describes John as leaning into Jesus (John 13:23–25), resting his head upon Jesus's chest, so near he could sense the rhythm of our Lord's heartbeat. John loved Jesus with all his heart and knew Jesus loved him just the same.

In that moment, John had no idea it would be his last meal with Jesus. No idea he would witness his beloved teacher's arrest, unjust trials, beatings, and crucifixion. No idea he would look upon his teacher's beaten and bloody body, hanging limp and lifeless from a criminal's cross.

But, the tide turned three days later. John walked into an empty tomb to discover Jesus had defeated death and risen from the grave (John 20:1–10)! And a few weeks after that beautiful resurrection moment, John's last glimpse of Jesus would be his beloved Savior, arms lifted toward the heavens, toes dangling from beneath his white robe, speaking words of blessing over His friends, ascending into the clouds (Luke 24:50).

"Then [Jesus] leads them out to Bethany. He lifts His hands and blesses them, and at that moment, with His hands raised in blessing, He leaves them and is carried up into heaven. They worship Him, then they return to Jerusalem, **filled with intense joy**, and they return again and again to the temple to celebrate God" (Luke 24:50–53 The Voice, emphasis added).

Don't miss Luke's words. John and the disciples returned to Jerusalem "filled with intense joy." I believe it's this unspeakable joy that fueled John's ministry for the remainder of his days. Despite decades of persecution and struggle, hard work and loneliness, John persevered. His love for Jesus and for the call God placed on his life never waned. His heart never wavered.

Over time, John's hair grayed. His skin bore the deep creases of his decades of serving and suffering for the One who had called him by name. John spent years recording the rich and treasured memories tucked deep in his heart and mind. Church tradition holds that he authored the gospel of John, the three epistles of John, and Revelation.[1]

As we begin our journey with John, we sense his deep and abiding joy in his opening words in 1 John chapter one.

Message from John's Heart to Ours

> **MEMORY VERSE:** *This is the message we have heard from him and declare to you: God is light; in him there is no darkness at all.* (1 John 1:5)

John opened his letter with these enduring words:

"We want to tell you about the One who was from the beginning. We have seen Him with our own eyes, heard Him with our own ears, and touched Him with our own hands. This One is *the manifestation of* the life-giving Voice, and He showed us **real life**, *eternal life*. We have seen it *all, and we can't keep what* we witnessed *quiet*—we have to share it with you. *We are inviting you to experience* eternal life through the One who was with the Father and came down to us" (1 John 1:1–2 The Voice, emphasis added).

John's words lay the foundation for faith in Jesus. A faith based on reality. A faith grounded in fact. Because he was an eyewitness to every word he wrote, his teaching is trustworthy. His experience real.

He courageously traveled, preached, and penned every word of his experiences to ensure Jesus's followers could know the same Jesus he knew. And so that you and I could know and believe in that same Jesus.

As you read his words, can't you sense his passion? The pleading in his voice? *Believe our words because we have seen Him. Touched Him. Heard Him. We walked with Him!* This One we followed, he says, spoke the voice of God.

Jesus gave John life. Real life. Everlasting life. Jesus loved John and the disciples in ways they had never experienced before. He performed miraculous wonders they had never seen before. He prophesied events that came to pass.

Digging Deeper

Read 1 John 1.

Understanding John's audience and the culture in which they lived is essential to understanding his letter. John wrote to the children of God . . . those who believed in Jesus.

Specifically, John wrote to embolden a declining church, a church he knew was compromising its beliefs. He didn't direct his letter to a specific church. Rather, he addressed it to all believers, using inclusive words like "my little children" and my "beloved."

He wrote with intentionality to expose the spreading virus of Gnosticism and the false teachers promoting it. What is Gnosticism? We'll dissect it more later. For our purposes now, it was a prominent movement counter to the Christian church, led by counterfeit Christians (false teachers) who had infiltrated the church.

In this day and age, how do we recognize a counterfeit Christian?

I first heard the term "counterfeit Christian" at a church in my hometown of Charlotte. The pastor centered his entire sermon on people who look like Christians, talk like Christians, but in the end, do not bear the marks of authenticity that belong to genuine believers in Jesus.

To bring it to a level to which we can easily relate, let's compare a counterfeit Christian with a counterfeit bill. Let's say you and I stop by our favorite pizza place for lunch. You treat and pay with a fifty-dollar bill. Amidst the change, you receive a twenty-dollar bill. It looks good to you. It looks good to me. And because you are a kind and generous mom, you give that twenty to your sixteen-year-old-daughter who just got her license. She uses it to buy gas and an Icee for herself and her friend. You *and* your daughter are such generous people! At the end of the day, the gas station manager takes that twenty-dollar bill, along with the rest of her cash from the till, to the bank and deposits it. At that point, one with greater knowledge about money than you, your daughter, and the gas station manager, rejects the bill.

You all used the twenty-dollar bill, and it remained in circulation until someone with specific knowledge identified it and exposed it for what it really was.

That's the way it is with counterfeit Christians. They show up in church on Sunday and play the part. To blend in, they speak the right words. They do the good deeds. But upon close examination, their hearts and lives don't line up with the truth of God's Word. Counterfeit teachers manipulate God's truth by leaving out the hard stuff of faith. They want more followers, so they don't want to exclude. And, because they want more power and control, they twist God's Word to fit their personal agenda.

Scripture is clear on the topic of counterfeit Christians. Matthew 7:21–23 says:

> *"Not everyone who says to me, 'Lord, Lord,' will enter the kingdom of heaven, but only the one who does the will of my Father who is in heaven. Many will say to me on that day, 'Lord, Lord, did we not prophesy in your name and in your name drive out demons and in your name perform many*

miracles?' Then I will tell them plainly, 'I never knew you. Away from me, you evildoers!'"

The frightening part about the counterfeit teachers in the early church—the Gnostics—was that they spoke of God, light, truth, and salvation but from their own philosophical and mystical interpretation. Their words sounded familiar. Sounded legitimate. But, when examined closely, the Gnostics approached these topics in radically different ways than Jesus. They twisted them for their own gain. They misled God's sheep.

For example, they advocated that Jesus never came in the flesh, that He was not human. They claimed that earthly matter is inherently bad and only the spirit is good. Because of that, anything done in the body, even the most horrific sin, had no meaning because real life existed only in the spirit. They also claimed that God is remote and distant from His creation, that He is pure and holy and cannot have anything to do with sinful and vile humanity.

John wrote his letter, in part, to expose and eradicate this heretical teaching.

Think of examples of counterfeit Christians today. Who are they and how do you recognize that they are counterfeit?

How do counterfeit Christians hurt the Christian church today?

In addition to issuing a warning about the Gnostics, John wrote this letter to invite the church into more intimate fellowship with one another and with God the Father and His Son. John knew the more closely knit their community, the less likely they would fall victim to the Gnostics' lies and deception. The more familiar they were with the truths of Scripture, the stronger their ability to stand against the false teachings and combat the doubts that accompany them.

Do you find this true for yourself? The more connected you are in church and Bible study, the more you can stand against the sway of the culture.

Give an example of when being in fellowship with believers has kept you from falling away from your faith.

_____

_____

_____

_____

_____

_____

Apply It

Read 1 John 1:4 and 3 John 1:4. List another reason John wrote his letter.

_____

_____

Joy marked John's ministry.

He deeply loved God and God's people. Shepherding and teaching brought him great joy. This joy fed his soul. John longed for everyone to know the joy, love, and fellowship that comes when believers come alongside each other in faith.

How does this carry over into our lives?

One of the distinguishing marks of an authentic believer is that she enjoys sharing the treasures she has received from knowing and loving God. She wants everyone she loves to experience the riches she has found in having a deep and abiding relationship with Jesus and with other believers. It makes her joy complete!

How are you sharing the riches of Christ with those around you?

_____

_____

_____

_____

Choose one person to encourage this week. Note his or her response to your encouragement, how it made you feel, and how God used it in your life and/or theirs.

_____

_____

_____

_____

_____

_____

_____

_____

Living in the Light

MEMORY VERSE: *This is the message we have heard from him and declare to you: God is light; in him there is no darkness at all.* (1 John 1:5)

The false teachers and teachings infiltrating the early church disturbed John greatly. So much so, that he addressed them in this letter one by one. He began with a big one. The Gnostics' teaching that those with unrepentant sin can still have intimate fellowship with God.

To answer this lie, John defined what it looks like to have fellowship with God, using not his own words but the words of Jesus.

"This is the message we have heard from him and declare to you: God is light; in him there is no darkness at all. If we claim to have fellowship with him and yet walk in the darkness, we lie and do not live out the truth. But if we walk in the light, as he is in the light, we have fellowship with one another, and the blood of Jesus, his Son, purifies us from all sin" (1 John 1:5–7).

1 John

What do you think it means when John says, "God is light"?

_____

_____

Jesus called Himself "the light" (John 8:12).

"When Jesus spoke again to the people, he said, 'I am the light of the world. Whoever follows me will never walk in darkness, but will have the light of life.'"

Who is Jesus, and what does He promise if we walk with Him?

_____

_____

John often referred to Jesus as light. We find some of his most powerful references in the opening message of his gospel:

"In the beginning was the Word, and the Word was with God, and the Word was God. He was with God in the beginning. Through him all things were made; without him nothing was made that has been made. In him was life, and that life was the light of all mankind. The light shines in the darkness, and the darkness has not overcome it.

"There was a man sent from God whose name was John. He came as a witness to testify concerning that light, so that through him all might believe. He himself was not the light; he came only as a witness to the light.

"The true light that gives light to everyone was coming into the world" (John 1:1–9).

"There was the true Light which, coming into the world, enlightens every man" (John 1:9 NASB).

Read John 1:1–9 quoted above. How many times do you find the word *light* in this passage?

_____

_____

What does John teach about the "light"?

_____

_____

Digging Deeper

It seems simple, right? If God is light, and we walk in the light, we will have fellowship with Him. So, all we need to do is walk in the light.

But walking in the light isn't easy. *Light* and *darkness* as used by John are not literal terms but moral terms. They speak of two contrasting natures: the nature of God and the nature of man. God is moral perfection—pure and holy. Man is moral imperfection—impure and sinful.

Let's step outside our lesson for a moment and go back to the beginning of Genesis to gain insight into sin. The moment Eve took and ate the fruit from the Tree of Knowledge of Good and Evil, sin corrupted humanity from that day forward, for every generation of people (Genesis 3). Paul explained the effect of that corruption in Romans 6:23: "[T]he wages of sin is death."

The Bible is clear: without Jesus, all people are steeped in sin and destined for death.

John 3:19 illustrates this same concept using light and darkness: "Light has come into the world, but people loved darkness instead of light because their deeds were evil." Light represents righteousness and goodness. Darkness represents evil and sin. We love darkness because of our imperfect sin nature. God abhors darkness because of His perfect sinless nature.

Friend, we must understand this truth before we can take one more step on our journey with John. By our very nature, we cannot stand in the presence of a holy God. We cannot on our own be in relationship with Him.

But God never abandons His children. Because of God's great love for us, He made a way to bring sinful man back into relationship with Him. A way in which we could once again stand before our Holy God.

It's the way of the blood-stained cross. This cruel Roman tool created for torture and death, in Jesus, defeats death and displays the fullness of God's love. Jesus, who lived the perfect, sinless life, died the death we deserve. A beautiful exchange. His perfect life for our imperfect life. His righteousness for our unrighteousness.

Jesus's single, grace-filled act restores our fellowship with God.

Now let's step back into our lesson. I walked us through the salvation message for foundational purposes, but John was not addressing salvation here. Remember, John wrote this letter to the church—to the "saved ones"—Christians who had already said yes to a relationship with Jesus. He was not concerned with their salvation. He was concerned with their daily walk.

Some in the church were choosing to walk in disobedience to God. In so doing, they chose to walk outside the fellowship they had gained at the cross. They were avoiding the light and immersing themselves deeper and deeper into sin and darkness.

I get it. I'm guilty of this. When I think certain thoughts, or behave in a certain way, hearing a sermon or reading my Bible can make me squirm. Why? Because light exposes darkness. The light of God's Word exposes my bad behavior. It shines a light on something I desperately try to hide.

A conversation with one of my Bible study girls brings this truth alive. For the last twelve years, I have taught Bible study here in Charlotte. One year, I invited a woman to join us. She seemed so eager. She showed up each week. But she never did her homework. I mean never. Everyone skips a week now and again for one reason or another, but she skipped consistently. I confess, it really upset me. As the teacher, I had spent hours researching, writing, and praying over the study and the questions. I believe with all my heart that life transformation flows from the time we invest *in* the Word, *not* from the teacher's lectures or commentary. It's sitting and soaking in our Bibles, allowing God to work in our hearts in and through the reading and the homework.

A few weeks into Bible study, I pulled this woman aside. I tenderly asked her why she didn't do her homework. She confessed that the few times she had opened her Bible in the past, it made her feel bad about herself. It made her see things about herself that she didn't like and didn't want to address or talk about.

That was not the answer I expected! Our conversation gave me a new perspective on our Bible study girls, especially the new ones. What this woman didn't know is that what she felt was conviction. Conviction from God's Holy Spirit. It was healthy and good. It was God's Hebrews 4:12 living and active Word coming alive in her heart, moving and penetrating it.

Oh, it's hard to come face-to-face with our sin. With our poor choices. With the ugliness that lurks in the deepest, darkest crevices of our hearts. But we must!

Are you turning from the light? Are there parts of you that still walk around in darkness? If yes, acknowledge and confess them.

_____

_____

Living in the light requires that our hearts, our actions, our words, our thoughts, our values, and even our schedules align with God's heart and His character, *not* with our sinful nature and fallen character.

Oh, how I fail at living in light . . . often. In fact, it happened smack in the middle of writing this study. Of course!

While writing this study, my husband and I traveled to New York City. The second day found us stranded in a downpour near Central Park, blocks and blocks from our hotel. With everyone trying to escape the deluge, cabs were scarce. We ran into the closest store to wait it out. But the rain continued. We decided to go for it, running in and out of stores, jumping over and around puddles. Soaked from head to toe, my patience wore thin. My husband and I exchanged words. You see, I suggested heading back as the first dark clouds rolled in. My husband disagreed and talked me into sticking it out. So, the "I told you so" attitude hijacked my heart. My words grew harsher, as did his. And then I stepped over the line. You may know that line. I spewed out words I knew cut to the core. Part of me wanted to take them back. To grab his hand, look in his eyes, and tell him how sorry I was. But the other side of me—the dark side—reasoned how valid they were in response to his words. Guess which side won out?

You guessed it!

We walked into our hotel room and sat in deafening silence. For hours, no words passed between us.

As I sat staring out the window, my eyes wandered to the bedside table. The light from the lamp illuminated my Bible. The words I had been studying on light and darkness flooded my mind. Sorrow engulfed my heart. I walked over to my husband, touched his shoulder, peeked my head around his, looked in his eyes, and asked for forgiveness. I thought it would be hard, but it wasn't. The illumination of God's Word penetrated my heart and melted it, literally melted it. My heart ached that my careless words had hurt my husband so deeply.

And although it took a few hours for my husband to fully surrender his hurt, he did. We enjoyed the rest of our time, experiencing the exciting sights and sounds of New York City, sans any more rain . . . or darkness!

We all sin. Every day. Many times a day.

Does that mean this whole light-and-dark thing creates a forever barrier with God? Can we ever have true fellowship? Can we ever stand in the presence of God fully comfortable, fully welcome?

Yes! Absolutely, yes! We can be comfortable in the presence of a holy God. John reminded us of this in verse 7 when he said the blood of Jesus purifies us from all unrighteousness. You see, God doesn't require sinless-ness . . . in fact, that's impossible. Only Jesus is sinless.

God doesn't require perfection. Only Jesus is perfect. God simply asks for repentance. When we repent of our sins, He forgives us fully and completely.

I love The Voice translation of John's words: "walk *step by step* in the light." Friend, it's a daily walk. But we don't walk alone. We walk with a loving, forgiving Father who empowers us through His Holy Spirit. He invites us to walk in the light. Of course, at times we may take a wrong step away from the light toward darkness. This misstep, if unacknowl-edged, will interrupt our fellowship with God. But the good news is, we need only turn our hearts back toward our heavenly Father and ask for-giveness. He waits with open arms!

And what about when we do mess up and mess up big?

All sin is equal. All sin has consequences. But the consequences are not equal.

Walking in the light continues as we agree with God about our sin. It's our refusal to agree with God about our sin that interrupts our fellow-ship with Him.

Let's examine the inner workings of sin for a minute.

Thoughts

Sin begins in our thoughts. Our thoughts lead us down the path of disobedience.

The first step to walking in the light is learning to interrupt our sinful thoughts *before* they lead us to action. It's taking action that truly inter-rupts our fellowship with God.

Walking in the light, daily sojourning with God, sensitizes our hearts to His Word and the leadings of His Holy Spirit. When we allow His Spirit to have His way in us, His Spirit convicts us of the tempting thoughts, the angry thoughts, the unforgiving thoughts and reminds us that they are unacceptable for one created in the image of God. As long as we respond to that conviction with obedience, fellowship remains.

What are some ways that you can ensure you walk step by step in the light?

_____

_____

If you find yourself in a place like I was in my hotel room that day, with your heart cracked in two . . . split down the middle . . . half in the dark, half in the light . . . be honest with God and with yourself. I'll let you in on a secret. God already knows your thoughts!

Read Psalm 139:1–6. What does this passage teach about the knowledge of God?

_____

_____

When we sense that conviction in our hearts, it's our loving Father intervening in our mess to draw us back to perfect fellowship with Him.

And don't miss two truths key to this teaching.

The Holy Spirit convicts. Conviction is good. It comes from the Father's heart of love. He is good. He is safe. He is trustworthy.

Satan condemns. He is not good. He is not safe. He is a liar and the father of lies. In him, there is no truth at all.

My friend, God never condemns. Romans 8:1 says, "Therefore, there is now no condemnation for those who are in Christ Jesus."

Thoughts Lead to Action

The Holy Spirit knows our thoughts. He knows our sinful thoughts will lead to sinful actions. His conviction interrupts those unholy thoughts and draws us back through His amazing grace. Agreeing with God about our sinful thoughts brings them into the light. It allows God to work in our hearts and minds to not only correct us but also train us to think, speak, and act in new ways. If we don't take immediate action to walk back into the light, we leave the door wide open for the enemy to take full control of the reins of our heart and lead us deeper into darkness and further into sin.

So, in that moment where we sense God's conviction, rather than allow pride to hold us hostage in the darkness, let's confess and agree with God about our sin and allow Him to move us into the light of His love and grace.

I've written a prayer we can pray the next time we find ourselves in this dilemma. I wish I had this prayer that day in New York City. My story would have read much differently. Make this prayer your own.

Thank You, Jesus, for speaking into my life right now. It's hard to hear Your convicting words. I'm still angry about what brought me here. But I confess I've allowed that anger and pride to hold me hostage. I agree with You in this moment that You are right and I am wrong. I no longer want these thoughts to fill my mind and these words to spew from my lips. Forgive me, Father. Renew my thoughts. Fill my heart and mind with thoughts that honor You and others. Lead me to my next steps so I know how to handle this situation in a way that honors and glorifies You and You alone.

Are you experiencing a battle in your heart right now? I encourage you to act today. Use this prayer as a starting point. Restore fellowship with your Father and then with anyone else you need to. Write your personal prayer below, along with any steps God leads you to take.

_____

_____

_____

And as a last step . . . maybe the most important step . . . accept your Father's forgiveness. Walk in the safety and security of His eternal, unchanging, everlasting love. Never forget that there is NO CONDEMNATION for those who are in Christ Jesus! As far as the east is from the west, that is how far God has removed our transgressions from us! (Psalm 103:12)

Read Psalm 119:30. What does the psalmist choose? Where do we find the way he has chosen?

_____

_____

Read Proverbs 6:20-21. According to Solomon, what should we do with God's teachings? What does it mean when it says, "fasten them [God's teachings] around your neck"? The Voice says, "engrave them on a pendant, and hang it around your neck."

_____

_____

Continue reading verses 22-23. What specifically does God's Word provide for us?

_____

_____

Read Psalm 19:8. What does this verse teach about God's Word and its role in our lives?

_____

_____

Apply It

John has now exposed the first of two diametrically opposed teachings that had been misleading and confusing his audience. We'll hear about the second teaching in the next section.

This first teaching claimed that those who intentionally choose to sin can maintain fellowship with God. John labeled this for what it was. A lie. We cannot maintain fellowship with a holy God if we continue to walk in darkness. To walk outside His will and His way. To accept the lies of the evil one as truth.

So, the moment we sense we are drifting away from the light and moving into darkness, we must change direction and walk back into the light. Below is a helpful script to follow when we find ourselves in this place. We must *choose* to:

♥ **interrupt** our thoughts,

♥ **confess** our sin,

♥ **turn around**, and

♥ **take a step** back into the light.

Step back into the light of His Word . . . His presence . . . Christian fellowship . . . praise and worship . . . Bible study . . . prayer.

Take some time to contemplate your fellowship with God. Do you find yourself walking more in the light or in the darkness? What choices do you need to make to walk more consistently in the light? Commit to take one step today to turn back to or assure you remain in God's light.

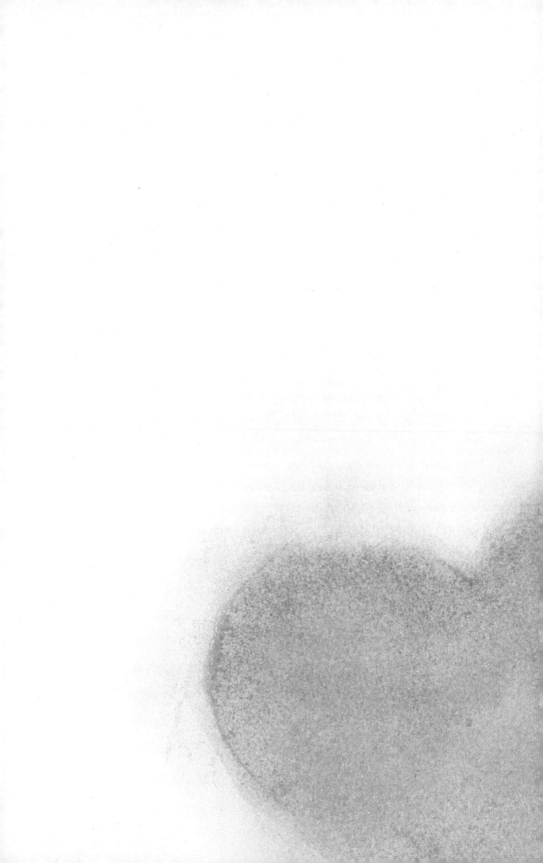

The Battle Within

MEMORY VERSE: *This is the message we have heard from him and declare to you: God is light; in him there is no darkness at all.* (1 John 1:5)

*H*ow are you coming along with your memory verse? This is the first of five verses you'll be hiding in your heart. Commit a little bit at a time to memory, and you'll have it memorized before you know it!

Digging Deeper

Read 1 John 1:8.

John takes this opportunity to address another false teaching, one that claimed once a person is saved, she is without sin. John labeled this lie for what it was and publicly denounced those who professed it.

"If we claim to be without sin, we deceive ourselves and the truth is not in us" (1 John 1:8).

Salvation—confessing our sin and inviting Jesus into our hearts—does not make us sinless. Sin will be our constant companion until

Jesus returns to rule and reign for all eternity! Then and only then will God transform us fully and completely into the flawless image in which He created us.

But the Gnostics taught otherwise. They led God's children to believe the lie that salvation—accepting Christ as their Savior—eradicated their sin nature and gave them a new, perfect nature.

This teaching is not biblical. Christians are not sinless. We are not perfect. Christians sin. We sin because, although we are saved, we still live in a fleshly body that seeks to satisfy its own desires. Jeremiah says it well, "The heart is deceitful above all things and beyond cure. Who can understand it?" (Jeremiah 17:9 NIV 1984).

As a saved child of God, yes, we receive a new nature. But that new nature lives inside our old body. Sometimes we succumb to our sinful nature even when we know it's wrong. We shift back to our old way of thinking; to that which is familiar and comfortable. Pride, lust, fear, anger, bitterness, jealousy, unforgiveness still struggle for control.

The capacity to sin remains as our two natures wrestle for power (Galatians 5:17). Sometimes our new nature prevails and sometimes, sadly, the old wins out.

Describe the places in your life where you experience this struggle.

_____

_____

The good news, my friend, is that this struggle within does *not* affect our salvation, our status in God's eyes. We are blood-bought daughters of the One True God. When we receive God's forgiveness and Christ's righteousness, it's for eternity. When God looks at us, He sees Jesus. It's our inheritance, and nothing can ever take it away.

Read John 10:28–29. These are Jesus's words. What do they speak to your heart?

_____

_____

God's beloved King David classically illustrates the battle within (2 Samuel 11–12). Remember God's name for David? "A man after [God's] own heart" (1 Samuel 13:14). But how can that be? In 2 Samuel 11, David violated not one but several of the Ten Commandments. He embarked on a notorious enterprise of sinful activity. He sinned in thought by lusting after another man's wife. He sinned in action when he sent for that woman and slept with her. Their illicit liaison resulted in a pregnancy.

Instead of openly confessing his sin, David schemed, not once but several times, to hide it. On his first attempt, David called the woman's husband, Uriah, back from the battlefield and encouraged him to sleep with his wife. That would have solved his problem, for sure. Uriah humbly refused. What an honorable man. One would think his noble response would have convicted David's heart. But it didn't.

Instead, David made another attempt to conceal his scandalous behavior. He invited Uriah to eat and drink with him. David "made him drunk," hoping Uriah would then go home and sleep with his wife. That plan failed as well.

As a last resort, David sent Uriah back to the battlefield, ordering his commander to send Uriah to the front lines to ensure he would be killed in combat.

Talk about interrupted fellowship! Not exactly a stellar example of a man who made wise, godly decisions.

David lied to God and to himself. He ignored his sin while attempting to carry on his royal duties. It was not until the prophet, Nathan, confronted David that he finally confessed. It took someone else holding him accountable to bring him to a place of repentance.

David's repentance restored his fellowship with God.

God forgave David because when, brought face-to-face with his sin, he humbled himself and confessed. Not just once but many times.

David's humility led God to honor David with a special title, a name for which he will be remembered for all time . . . a man after God's own heart.

Never forget, friend, nothing and no one can ever take away your promise of eternal life. Jesus bought it at a great price. Not even Satan can steal it!

However, our sin does interrupt our fellowship with God. And although God forgave David's sin, it did not erase the consequences of that sin. But that is another story for another day.

To summarize . . .

We are fallen people, with a fallen nature that leads us to sin.

That sin interrupts our fellowship with God.

We are also a saved people, indwelled with God's Spirit who empowers us to obey.

We have two sets of desires warring within us, so it comes down to choices. God gives us freedom to choose. We can choose to walk in the light and live in its glorious radiance, or we can choose to succumb to temptation and slither off into the darkness. It's those choices that move us toward the light or away from the light.

Read Galatians 5:16–23.

How do verses 16–18 in this passage support John's teachings? What is the key to conquering sinful desires?

_____

_____

What is the poison fruit of our sinful nature? (See verses 19-21; Romans 1:29–31.)

_____

_____

What is the blessed fruit of our new nature? (See verses 22–23.)

_____

_____

John made it very clear. There is no perfect new nature! We sin. But God, through His Holy Spirit, empowers us to overcome that sin.

It begins with a submissive, obedient heart. It requires day-by-day, step-by-step obedience.

Read Galatians 5:24–26. What are some keys to keeping "in step" with the Spirit in this battle?

_____

_____

Apply It

The Lie:

We are sinless.

Those who taught this twisted truth were fooling themselves and were "strangers to the truth" (1 John 1:8 The Voice). John makes it clear that if we claim to be without sin, we "deceive ourselves and the truth is not in us" (1:8).

The Truth:

We are not sinless.

In Jesus, we are forgiven. We are redeemed. We are empowered.

And as we draw closer to Jesus and walk in the radiance of His light, His Word and His Spirit heighten our awareness of the darkness. Words we spoke and actions we took that never bothered us before feel uncomfortable, maybe even shameful.

God knew this, and that's why He gave us His promise in 1 John 1:9. Don't undervalue the wonderful promises found in this verse, which we'll study in the next section.

Before we close, take a few minutes to work on your memory verse.

God Is Faithful to Forgive

> **MEMORY VERSE:** *This is the message we have heard from him and declare to you: God is light; in him there is no darkness at all.* (1 John 1:5)
>
> **W**e are nearing the end of our first week! Let's summarize what we have learned so far.
>
> ♥ God invites us into an intimate relationship with Him.
>
> ♥ God desires for us to be comfortable in His presence.
>
> ♥ The key to this comfort is walking in the light and avoiding darkness.
>
> ♥ Those who claim to have fellowship with God but who simultaneously walk in darkness, lie.
>
> ♥ Those who claim sinlessness based on salvation are deceived.[2]
>
> John has taught us about counterfeit Christians, false teachers, and their false claims. He presented biblical truths to combat their

lies. Here, in 1 John 1:9, John stops debating and presents the beauty of the gospel:

"But if we own up to our sins, God shows that He is faithful and just by forgiving us of our sins and purifying us from the pollution of all the bad things we have done" (The Voice).

Friend, the bottom line is grace.

Our fellowship with God is not contingent upon our sinlessness but upon His forgiveness.

Let me say that again. Our fellowship with God is not contingent upon our sinlessness but on His forgiveness.

The incredible reality of grace is that even though we are imperfect, even though we sin, even though we disappoint God daily, He still loves us and makes a way for us to remain in fellowship with Him!

Digging Deeper

John asks us to "own up to our sins." Other translations use the word *confess* (NIV). To confess simply means "to acknowledge." The Greek word here is *homologeo*, which means "to speak the same thing."[3] Owning up to our sin or confessing our sin is not a simple apology. It's not a quick "I'm sorry."

Confession is acknowledging our sin and agreeing with God that it really is a sin, not making excuses for it or justifying it.

I am so good at the second part . . . justifying my sin. How about you?

If you and I are truly serious about walking closer with the Lord, we must be willing to see our sin for what it is, confess it, and allow God's refining process to do its work in us. Malachi 3:2–3 says:

"But who can endure the day of his coming? Who can stand when he appears? For he will be like a refiner's fire or a launderer's soap. He will

sit as a refiner and purifier of silver; he will purify the Levites and refine them like gold and silver."

God's ways are not our ways. Seldom does being immersed in a fire ever result in anything other than utter destruction, loss, and death. The dark days following 9/11, forever etched in our minds, revealed the all-consuming destructive power of fire.

Proverbs 25:4 says, "Take away the impurities from the silver, and a *good* smith can create something *of value*" (The Voice).

The King James translation says, "Take away the dross from the silver, and there shall come forth a vessel for the finer."

Dross is defined as waste matter, refuse, that which is worthless and of no value.[4] In this process, fire consumes dross and brings to the surface the impurities of that which is being burned.

Malachi 3:2 describes God as a "refiner's fire." Hebrews describes God as a "consuming fire" (12:29). "He is like a fierce fire that consumes everything" (The Voice). God's holy fire consumes our dross . . . our flesh . . . our human desires . . . our secret sin. When we are intentional about walking in the light, it's imperative that we invite God to excise what is unholy so He can unveil what is holy.

Malachi 3:2 also compares God to lye soap. The ESV says God is like "fullers' soap." I was not familiar with this term, so I looked it up. A *fuller* was someone who cleaned and thickened freshly woven (usually woolen) cloth. His chief task was cleansing and whitening garments for festive and religious occasions. White garments typify Christ's righteousness.[5]

The cleansing process involved cleaning, bleaching, wetting, and beating the fibers to a consistent and desirable condition. Fullers' soap was the strong, lye-based soap the fuller used to bleach the impurities from the new cloth.

And why the name "fuller"? It came from the actual field by that name referenced in the Old Testament (2 Kings 18:15–17, Isaiah 36:1–2), an area west of Jerusalem where the fullers cleaned and bleached the woolen cloth. They washed the cloth with the soap and then placed it on rocks and beat it with sticks until it was free of all impurities.[6]

Both the refining process and the fullers' soap process stressed thoroughness and severity.

It's a bit frightening that God compares His work in our lives to a consuming fire and the laborious and arduous cleansing work of the fuller. But in the hands of a loving God who wants only our highest and best, we can trust His process. We can trust that His refining and cleansing methods draw us closer to His heart and work toward conforming us into the image in which He created us.

This process makes it more important that we agree with God about our sin. If we don't, we erect a barrier between ourselves and God. God took care of our sin on the cross. He died for all our sins . . . past, present, and future.

However, this truth does not give us license to sin. The crimson stain of sin interrupts fellowship with our Savior. It's the confession of our sin, the admitting and taking responsibility of it, that opens the way for God's mercy and grace to flood our hearts and wash away every crimson stain so that not even a blush of color remains.

We are washed white as snow (Isaiah 1:18). The Voice says, "*made clean again* like *new* wool."

Confession accomplishes above and beyond restoring fellowship. It gets us on our knees and reminds us of who we are and who God is. It aligns our hearts with His and makes us pliable so He can sculpt us into the women He created us to be. It purges shame and condemnation. It ushers in freedom and renewed fellowship with our Creator and Father!

Are you struggling with a sin today? Join me in walking through a time of confession.

Find a quiet place.

Prepare your heart by offering up praise and thanksgiving to your Father in heaven.

Admit your sin and agree with God about that sin.

Confess your sin.

Receive God's forgiveness!

Reread 1 John 1:9. What promise is yours after you receive your Father's forgiveness?

_____

_____

God's promise in 1 John 1:9 begins with forgiveness, but it ends with something richer and greater. Purification. He purifies our hearts. God's grace reaches into the deepest, darkest spaces and unearths our hidden motives and desires. Over time, His grace shifts and shapes us into the gloriously beautiful image in which we were created. His image.

Let's spend a few minutes with Paul and dig a bit deeper into the topics of sin and temptation.

Read 1 Corinthians 10:1–13.

What story does Paul share in verses 1–4?

_____

_____

_____

List the sins of the Israelites in verses 6–10.

_____

_____

_____

What does Paul say was the reason these things occurred (verses 6, 11)?

_____

_____

_____

What is Paul's warning in verse 12?

_____

_____

What does Paul teach us about temptation in verse 13?

_____

_____

What is God's promise in that verse?

_____

_____

Temptation itself is not a sin. Jesus was tempted. YIELDING to the temptation . . . that is the sin.

Describe a time of temptation. How did God provide a means of escape? Did you take it?

_____

_____

What is your "go to" strategy when you are being tempted?

_____

_____

Apply It

God calls us to walk and live in the light . . . to be holy as He is holy. It sounds impossible, but with God it's totally possible. He created us in His image and, thankfully, He doesn't see us as we see ourselves. He sees beyond our sin, beyond our human frailties. He sees the woman He created us to be and the potential we have.

Walking in the light equips us to become that woman.

Walking in fellowship with Christ, day-by-day, step-by-step, ensures we live a life set apart from the world in our thoughts and actions. Ensures that we walk a consistent walk, one in which who we *say* we are and who we *really* are match.

God's way requires . . .

💜 intentional choices.

💜 knowing truth so we can identify lies.

💜 turning away from darkness and walking toward the light.

💜 agreeing with God about our sin.

💜 humbly confessing our sin.

💜 complete dependence upon Him.

💜 refusing to yield to temptation.

Sin is inevitable. Temptation happens.

But we are never alone. God is ever present. He indwells and empowers us. He equips us with spiritual discernment to alert us to the people and situations seeking to lead us away from the light and into darkness. His Spirit provides the courage to resist temptation and to stand firm on the truth. His Spirit opens the line of communication so we can cry out in prayer and hear His answer and leading.

What steps do you need to take to be a woman known by her godly actions and not her sinful reactions?

_____

_____

_____

_____

_____

Group Discussion Questions

1. John had the privilege of being the last man standing, the last living apostle to speak for God. He spent those last days standing strong in God's Word, proclaiming the truth about Jesus, and inviting his listeners into true fellowship with Him.

   a. What does it look like for us today to stand firm and hold fast to the Word of God?

   b. What are ways we can invite others into our faith walk and into true fellowship with Jesus?

2. Do you have a person in your life for whom you are praying to come to know Jesus?

   a. If so, in what ways are you living to make Jesus appealing and inviting?

   b. Share a step (or two) you are willing to take to come alongside that person and join God in His work to answer your prayer.

3. This week we talked about the distinguishing marks of a believer. I shared how I lacked patience and self-control (two fruit of the Spirit). Evidence of God's fruit (love, joy, peace, patience, kindness, goodness, gentleness, faithfulness, and self-control) is a beautiful mark of a believer.

   a. Choose one fruit you feel marks your life. How does the presence of that fruit encourage others and draw others to you and to Jesus?

   b. Choose one fruit (yes, only one) you lack. What are some ways you can work with the Lord to increase the presence of that fruit in your life? If you have time, find a few Scriptures to pray and personalize, as I talked about in the video.

4. God calls us to stand up for truth, even when it's hard and makes us uncomfortable (like my friend did at her dinner party). He asks us to represent our faith well. To take our faith to deeper more mature places.

   a. What steps are you taking toward this kind of maturity?

   b. Do you hear God's voice as my friend did? If so, how does He speak to you? If not, what can you do to ensure His voice intersects with your everyday life?

   c. Share a few Scriptures you have tucked in your heart so you can recall them the moment you need them. If you don't have any, choose one or two to memorize.

5. At the end of the video, I invited you to take one step to live out what you have learned today. What step will you take?

WALK IN OBEDIENCE

PRAYER: *Heavenly Father, thank You for all that You have taught me about Your Son as the Light of the World. I want to walk in the Light and shine Your Light to those around me. I know that this requires obedience on my part. My heart longs to be obedient, yet I struggle sometimes with obeying. I want my own way and I let my feelings lead rather than Your Spirit. Give me listening ears and a softened heart. Grant me a willing spirit, a submissive spirit to sustain me and carry me through each day. Give me grace to obey even when it's difficult, inconvenient, or against everything I want to do. Help me to honor You with my choices, my words, and my actions. Enable me through the power of Your Holy Spirit to obey even when it costs me. Day by day, help me grow in obedience and, through my obedience, draw me closer to Your heart and deeper in Your love. I ask this in Jesus's name. Amen.*

We Have an Advocate

> **MEMORY VERSE:** *We know that we have come to know him if we keep his commands.* (1 John 2:3)

Read 1 John 2.

Now that you've come to know John better, I wonder if you've noticed something unique about his writing style. I've noticed oft-repeated words and themes:

- ♥ light and dark
- ♥ truth and lies
- ♥ true teaching and false teaching
- ♥ the new command and the old command
- ♥ love and hate
- ♥ loving the Father and loving the world
- ♥ Christ and antichrist

John expertly analyzed, and used contrasts to highlight, the differences between *real* Christians and the counterfeit Christians infiltrating the church.

Yet, as he exposed lies and liars with great command and authority, John wrote with a tender, loving heart. He's a beautiful model of how to live God's command to speak truth in love (Ephesians 4:15).

With what words does John open 1 John 2?

_____

_____

By the time John penned these words, his feet had traversed many miles. That passage of time transformed him. It softened his heart. The way he addressed his audience reflects this change. He called them "my dear children." In Jesus's time, teachers used similar terminology (*teknion* in the Greek) to address their disciples, especially in circumstances that required tenderness.[7] John considered believers his spiritual children who needed not only education but also clarification about the foundational beliefs of their faith.

It wasn't that John questioned their faith, because they already believed in Jesus. But they needed equipping to live out that faith. They lacked the truth needed to combat the lies infiltrating their churches. If we're honest, we find the same problem in the church today.

Digging Deeper

In the first few verses of chapter 2, John reminded his audience why he wrote this letter . . . so that they may not sin. But in his very next breath, knowing every one of them would sin, he shared the good news!

What is the good news John shared in verses 1 and 2?

_____

_____

The thing about sin? It rarely travels alone. It brings with it unwelcome traveling companions like shame and guilt. They announce their arrival something like this: *There you go again. You'll never change. Why do you even try? You'll never be good enough. God could never use you.*

Sound familiar? Sometimes these lies stick around longer than the sin itself.

Before we go any further, is there a sin from your past for which you have experienced shame and guilt? Where did that sin and those emotions leave you?

_____

_____

_____

_____

_____

I don't know about you, but I often welcome these lies with open arms. Help, hope, and healing come only when we identify the lies and expose sin's unwelcome accomplices.

From where do the lies come?

Our sworn enemy, Satan. He has many names. John identified Satan as "**the accuser** . . . who accuses them before our God day and night. . . ." (Revelation 12:10, emphasis added). Jesus gave him two more names in John 8:44: "he [Satan] cannot tolerate the truth because he is void of anything true. At the core of his character, he is a **liar**; everything he speaks originates in these lies because he is the **father of lies**" (The Voice, emphasis added).

John took this opportunity to unmask Satan and to arm God's children with the truth about who he really is. He reminded them that they do not fight their enemy alone. They had an Advocate.

And so do we!

His name is Jesus.

Let's bring this to the real world for a minute. After my second year of law school, I had the honor of interning in our city's District Attorney's office. It was exciting, but challenging, dealing with lawyers, judges, and criminals day in and day out. One case stands out among all the rest. It involved parents who had sexually abused their two young daughters. Witness testimony revealed repulsive acts that turned my stomach. And if the abuse wasn't enough, these so-called parents documented their horrific crimes in a photo album.

The deeper we delved into the facts, it became clear that this monster who masqueraded as a husband and father had threatened and coerced his wife into participating. To convict the husband to the highest extent allowed by law, we needed to work a deal with the wife to secure her testimony against him.

The wife retained her own attorney, and we negotiated the deal. With her lawyer by her side, she stood before the judge and pled guilty to lesser crimes, enabling us to go after her husband with the full force of the law. Presented with the photo album and the testimony of the mother and oldest daughter, the jury found her husband guilty. The judge threw down the gavel and sentenced him to life in prison.

Just as the mother of those children needed and retained an advocate to stand alongside her as she stood before the judge, we too have an Advocate. But we don't have just any defense attorney. We have the best defense attorney in the universe standing alongside us, pleading our case. Our Advocate is the Judge's own Son! Jesus. He suffered for our crime. He paid for it at the cross. He took our place.

Do you know what that means, my friend? It means that we can never be tried for our sins again. Jesus paid the price once and for all.

It is finished. Done.

Jesus stands before God as our mediator. In Him, we are forgiven and purified!

No matter the lies Satan fires at us. No matter the unwelcome traveling companions he sends our way. Jesus's death and resurrection threw down the gavel once and for all!

Game over.

Satan loses every time.

Apply It

The liar. The father of lies. The accuser wants us to believe the Judge continually picks up the gavel every time we do wrong, but He doesn't.

Let the power of this truth sink in.

None of us, no matter what we have done, is beyond the reach of Jesus's forgiveness.

Not one. That includes you, and it includes me. Jesus died for every single one of us. All we must do is turn from our sin, confess it, and receive Jesus's forgiveness. Whether it's for the first time . . . for our salvation, or for our daily sins. Jesus is enough!

Are you holding on to a sin right now? Take it to your Advocate.

Hear these words from the Judge, your Father in heaven, declared over you now:

"You are forgiven!"

Place your name in the blank below:

_____ , *My child whom I love and adore, My child for whom My Son gave His life . . . YOU ARE FORGIVEN!*

Speak these words out loud. Speak them and believe them.

They are truth and the truth will set you free!

Obedience

MEMORY VERSE: *We know that we have come to know him if we keep his commands.* (1 John 2:3)

*I*f you spend any time around young children, you know bedtime is a struggle, and it was no different with my youngest. When we announced bedtime, Monty and I expected obedience. But that wasn't what we always got. Bo inevitably wanted to stay up as late as possible. Excuses abounded as bedtime drew closer. *I want a drink of water. One more story. My stomach hurts. I'm scared.* His failure to obey always resulted in unpleasant consequences, but they never seemed to faze him.

Much of John's message centers around this topic of obedience.

Define obedience in your own words.

_____

_____

Three actions motivate us to obey. We *have* to. We *need* to. We *want* to.

Slaves have to obey. If they fail to obey their masters, severe consequences ensue. Beatings. Torture. Even death.

Employees need to obey. If they fail to obey, guaranteed consequences follow. Monetary loss. Reduction in responsibility or hours. Even loss of employment.

But with believers, it's different. We obey not because we have to or need to but because we want to. We love God, and pleasing Him becomes the desire of our heart.

Digging Deeper

John's words in 1 John 2:3 are profound.

Write verse 3 below.

_____

_____

How do we know that we have come to know God intimately?

_____

_____

John uses the word *know* more than twenty times in 1 John alone. It follows that it is a key concept and one we must understand.

The Greek word for *know*, as used here, is *ginosko*, which means "grasping the full reality and nature of an object under consideration."[8] John wrote this letter to people who knew *about* Jesus but did not really *know* Jesus personally and intimately. They had head knowledge of Him (impersonal) but not heart knowledge (intimate). And their head knowledge was often tainted by the false teachers within the church.

John wrote, in part, to teach his spiritual children (and us) that there is more to knowledge than familiarity with facts.

Authentic knowledge is also experiential. We gain deeper, more intimate knowledge when we open our hearts to Jesus, spending time with Him day in and day out . . . praying, studying, listening, worshiping.

Over time, our head knowledge moves into our hearts. It becomes personal. Intimate.

Read John 10:1–5 and 10:27. What do these verses teach?

_____

_____

This is a perfect parable for this lesson. Sheep know the voice of their shepherd because he cares for them and leads them day after day. Even when he leaves them in a sheepfold for the night, mixed with sheep belonging to other shepherds, the sheep will not come when called by other shepherds. They come only when they hear the voice of *their* shepherd.

It's no different with us. One of Jesus's names is the "good shepherd" (John 10:14). The more time we spend with our Shepherd, Jesus, the more familiar His voice. It rises above other voices that clamor for our attention and affection. We come to trust that voice. Believe that voice. And eventually, respond in obedience to that voice.

It's this intimate knowledge of Jesus that transforms and softens *our hearts* to trust and obey Him.

And let's be clear. John is not saying we know God by *doing*. That leads to a works-based faith.

He's saying that we *know* (with certainly and confidence) that we know God when we obey His commands. It's a heart issue. Do you see the difference?

Let's dig a bit deeper into this teaching grammatically. In the Greek, John wrote, "we know [present tense] that we know Him [perfect tense]." *Keep up with me here in the grammar lesson.* The present tense means our knowing is now, while the perfect tense means something that happened in the past with results that continue into the future. The perfect tense is literally translated "we have known Him, and continue to know Him." John is saying, "We know today that we came to know Him in the past and continue to know Him in the present if we keep His commandments."[9]

Paul used the same Greek perfect tense of "be" in Colossians 3:10 when he wrote, "put on the new self, which is being renewed in knowledge in the image of its Creator." *Renewed* here is essentially translated "be being renewed"—it is both an active and constant experience.

And let me repeat what we learned in Week 1. This teaching is not about salvation. When we accept Jesus as our Lord and Savior, salvation is ours. Period. Salvation places us into the family of God. An eternal union that is ours always and forever.

This teaching is about *sanctification*, God's process of making us holy and more like Him as we walk in the light with Him and live out our salvation. Walking with Jesus, spending time with Him every day, that is how we become more like Him. It's what Christians call fellowship. And that, not salvation, is what's at issue here.

The longer we walk with Jesus, the easier obedience becomes.

And relating back to last week's lesson, daily walking in obedience helps maintain our fellowship with God.

Disobedience interrupts that fellowship. Dr. David Jeremiah says it well,

> *Here's an important distinction: Our union with Christ is demonstrated by our communion with Christ, but it is not dependent upon our communion with Christ. We don't lose our union with Christ by sinning and not immediately confessing. But when our communion is strong we do hold up a sign to the world that says, "I am in union with God Almighty. I am a part of the family of God."* [10]

Another commentator writes, "John does not suggest that relationship with God is *established* by obedience; rather, that relationship is *demonstrated* by obedience." [11]

Don't miss that. Relationship is demonstrated by obedience.

Read John 14:15. How does this verse speak to what John is saying here regarding obedience?

_____

_____

Thankfully, my friend, the standard of obedience that John speaks of is not perfect obedience. God looks for women whose hearts are responsive to His Word. Whose hearts seek to honor God in all they say and do *to the best of their ability*. And when we make a mistake, when we disobey or disappoint God, we repent and turn our hearts back toward Him.

Back to my sweet boy, Bo. As he matured, his motivation for obedience did as well. Initially, Bo obeyed because he knew disobedience resulted in unpleasant consequences, like a timeout or even a spanking. He didn't like that, so he obeyed to avoid the consequences. In his elementary and middle school years, he obeyed because if he didn't, he lost privileges. No playing with friends. No allowance. Extra chores. Now that he is a young man, he obeys more out of love and the desire to please and honor his parents. Of course, Bo's obedience is not perfect, and sometimes it's delayed, but we have witnessed a clear change in his heart as he grows and matures.

And this is how it is with us. We obey God early on, maybe out of the misguided fear of punishment (have to) or the motive that when we do, we will be rewarded (need to). But as we grow in our knowledge of God through intimate time with Jesus, we experience Him more personally, and we desire to honor and please Him in all that we do.

John then writes some difficult words in 1 John 2:4.

Write verse 4 below. What strong language does he use here?

_____

_____

If a person says she knows God but does not keep His commands, John calls it like it is. That person is a liar. There is no truth in her. Sounds harsh, doesn't it?

It isn't. John writes these defining words to ensure his spiritual children know exactly what truly knowing God requires.

In verse 5, John presents the other side of the coin: "But if someone *responds to and* obeys His word, then God's love has truly taken root and filled Him" (1 John 2:5 The Voice). The NIV says, "But if anyone obeys his word, love for God is truly made complete in them."

When we walk in obedience to God's Word, God's love is truly made complete in us. It implants itself into the soil of our hearts and takes root. It then blooms and grows, expanding and filling our hearts like a balloon. The King James translation says the love of God is "perfected" in us. This word *perfected* in the Greek is *teleioo* and means "to make perfect, to consummate in character, to consecrate."

Obedience proves the reality of God's love is actively at work within us.

And, thankfully, we don't have to produce obedience on our own. God's Holy Spirit enables and empowers us to obey. The moment we accept Jesus as our Lord and Savior, God seals us with His Holy Spirit. God Himself indwells us and, through His presence in us, we receive the fruit of that Spirit.

Read Galatians 5:22–23. What is the fruit of God's Spirit?

_____

_____

As we grow in our relationship with Jesus, that fruit, one being God's love, overtakes our hearts and manifests itself in our lives. This overtaking is not a one-time occurrence. It's a filling process. God perfects His love in us over time. And the more we choose obedience, the more perfect our love becomes.

John ends this portion of Scripture in verse 6.

Read 1 John 2:6. When we live in intimacy with Jesus, what should we do?

_____

_____

How do we know what it means to live like Jesus?

_____

_____

Describe what this looks like in your life.

_____

_____

In families, we look to older siblings and parents for wisdom and advice. We watch to see how they act and respond. We then model what we observe. It's no different in God's family. We look to Jesus, God manifest in the flesh, as our example . . . our role model.

Tying this back to Week 1 and John's call to walk in the light, what does that look like? How do we know how to walk in the light?

It means living the way Jesus lived when He walked the earth. And how do we know how Jesus lived? We look to God's Word. It is through studying the stories and listening to the words of Jesus found between Matthew and Acts that we discover how Jesus reacted and responded, and are commanded to do the same.

Let's give it a try. How should we respond when someone betrays us?

Travel to the book of Luke with me and read some of Jesus's most profound words on this topic, spoken from the agony of the cross. Looking into the faces of those who had persecuted, whipped, mocked, and nailed Him to the cross, He spoke these words to His Father, "Father, forgive them, for they do not know what they are doing" (Luke 23:34).

That's our answer. It's crystal clear. Amid ultimate betrayal, Jesus forgave. Paul's writings bolster Jesus's words: "Be kind and compassionate to one another, forgiving each other, just as in Christ God forgave you" (Ephesians 4:32).

I'm not saying this is easy, because it's not. Forgiving a mother for walking out on her children. Forgiving a murderer for taking the life of a family member. Forgiving a father for sexually abusing his child. Forgiving a spouse for betraying a marriage vow. All scenarios seem unimaginable. Yet, when we acknowledge and remember everything for which we have been forgiven, it should come a bit easier. And, it's what Christ calls us to do because He knows what's best for us. When we refuse to forgive, unforgiveness wraps its ugly tentacles around our fragile hearts, choking out every ounce of peace, joy, and hope. Failing to forgive also distances us from experiencing forgiveness.

When we walk in the light . . . when we walk as Christ walked . . . it not only changes our hearts, it transforms our homes and our relationships. Think of the issues that arise in your everyday, walking around lives. Without fail, God's Word, from Genesis to Revelation, speaks to them. It might be through a truth, a promise, a directive, a commandment, a story, or a psalm.

God doesn't stop at His Word. He also communicates with us through:

♥ His Spirit

♥ His creation

♥ His people

♥ Worship

♥ Life's circumstances

♥ Prayer

Friend, our ability to obey, to honor God in all we say and do comes much more easily when we walk in the light, when we maintain close fellowship with Him. Intimate fellowship readies our hearts to receive the fullness of God's blessings and positions us perfectly for Him to live out His light and love through us.

Let's celebrate today! Note some ways that walking in the light—obeying God's Word—has changed your heart and your home. It's a great equipping tool for us to have some "go to" Scriptures to help with the challenges we face at work and at home. If you are doing this study in a group, gather the Scriptures that helped you and share them with the group.

_____

_____

_____

_____

Love One Another

MEMORY VERSE: *We know that we have come to know him if we keep his commands.* (1 John 2:3)

Love. A simple four-letter word that elicits deep emotion, generates genuine heartache, inspires catchy tunes, and transforms lives.

Note one or two of your favorite song lyrics/titles that talk about love (i.e., "Can't Buy Me Love"). And if you really want to challenge yourself, name the artist (the Beatles). Okay, mine was easy.

Read 1 John 2:7–11.

Digging Deeper

John again opens by tenderly addressing his audience, "Dear friends, I am not writing you a new command but an old one, which you have had since the beginning. This old command is the message you have heard" (1 John 2:7).

1 John

Read Deuteronomy 6:5 and Leviticus 19:18. What is the old command?

_____

_____

Moving to the New Testament, let's look at how Jesus responded when asked, "Which is the greatest commandment in the Law?" (Matthew 22:36).

Read Matthew 22:37–40. Write the main points of Jesus's response.

_____

_____

Loving God and loving neighbor have been part of God's law for centuries. John wasn't changing the law. Instead, he was calling his audience, and us, to put the old commandment into practice in a fresh, new way.

Let's explore the original language for a moment and engage in a word study. The Greeks had two different words for *new*. One meant "new in time," and the other "new in quality." To illustrate this distinction, let's compare two cars. The first "new" (new in time) would describe the most recent model of a car. But the second "new" (new in quality) would describe the latest and greatest high-tech concept car that radically differs from all other cars. The New Testament command to love one another is not new in time, but it *is* new in quality.[12]

Jesus elevated love above the other commands of which He had spoken because love is the fulfillment of all the other commands.

Familiarize yourself with the Ten Commandments (Exodus 20:1–17 or Deuteronomy 5:6–21).

All Ten Commandments are grounded in love. The first four command us to love God and instruct us how to do so. The last six command us to love others and demonstrate how to live this out.

Bottom line: God's Ten Commandments teach us how to love.

The old command to "love one another" took on new meaning in John 13:34 with Jesus's words: "So I give you a new command: Love each other *deeply and fully.* Remember the ways that I have loved you, and demonstrate your love for others in those same ways" (The Voice).

The fruit of the Spirit, of which love is one—implanted in us the moment we invite Jesus into our hearts—not only equips us to love God deeply and fully but also equips us to love others in the same way.

Obeying God's commands, doing the right thing, is no longer simply a matter of law as it was in the Old Testament. It's now a matter of love. When we love our parents with Jesus's love, we desire to honor them. When we love our neighbor, we won't covet their belongings. When we love our employer, we won't steal from him.

Now, I must confess, there are times when that kind of love doesn't come naturally for me! It's easy to talk about Christian love, but oh so hard sometimes to practice it. Years ago, in fact my first job out of college, I worked for a woman who could not have been more difficult. She was not my direct boss. But, because I worked in an administrative position, she often hijacked me to do menial tasks around the office that no one else wanted to do. With her, everything had to be done immediately and to her exact standards, no matter if I had a pressing assignment from my direct boss. I dreaded going to work every day. I knew law school was only months away and I would be leaving soon, but it didn't change my negative attitude. This woman was undeniably difficult to like, let alone love.

If only I had known then what I know now, perhaps my time at that company would have been different. Since that job, I've had more difficult employers—not many, but a few. The difference? Faith now enters the picture. A heart transformed by Jesus guides my actions and reactions. I now have an arsenal of truths and promises to pray and a love flowing through me that I have finally learned how to access.

Friend, Christian love is not a shallow, sentimental emotion. It's not a feeling we muster in our own strength. It's a matter of will. It's resolving in our mind to love others the way Jesus loved others and the way God loves us. It's a matter of obedience.

There's no better way to describe the legs of living out this love than Paul's words in 1 Corinthians 13:

> *Love never gives up.*
> *Love cares more for others than for self.*
> *Love doesn't want what it doesn't have.*
> *Love doesn't strut,*
> *Doesn't have a swelled head,*
> *Doesn't force itself on others,*
> *Isn't always "me first,"*
> *Doesn't fly off the handle,*
> *Doesn't keep score of the sins of others,*
> *Doesn't revel when others grovel,*
> *Takes pleasure in the flowering of truth,*
> *Puts up with anything,*
> *Trusts God always,*
> *Always looks for the best,*
> *Never looks back,*
> *But keeps going to the end.*
> (The Message)

Jeremiah weighed in on this topic as well. He prophesied the difference between the old and the new command in Jeremiah 31:33–34.

Read Jeremiah's words. What does he say?

_____

_____

_____

Now, instead of God's Ten Commandments being inscribed in stone, God has woven them into the fabric of our hearts. They become a part of who we are . . . living, breathing words at work within us.

In commanding us to love, Jesus is not asking us to do anything He hasn't already done or anything He has not equipped us to do. He not only planted His love in us but also modeled it for us. Jesus's life exemplified one long walk of love amid some of the most difficult circumstances and unlovable people. He never displayed hatred or malice. And although His righteousness hated all sin and disobedience, He never hated the people who committed those sins. A strong and beautiful undercurrent of love motivated all He did.

Jesus deeply loved His twelve disciples despite their bickering, unbelief, disobedience, and jockeying for position. In so doing, He modeled the life of love they were to imitate after He was gone.

Jesus loved beyond His inner circle. He loved the sinners, the tax collectors, the commoners, the poor, the outcast, the sick, the children, the elderly, and everyone in between, even the thief on the cross. And probably most shocking and hard to accept, Jesus loved His enemies . . . those who mocked and persecuted Him, those who betrayed Him.

John closed this portion of Scripture drawing us back to light and darkness.

Read 1 John 2:9–10. What does this passage speak to you about love and living in the Light?

_____

_____

The word _hate_, as used here, is from the Greek word _miseo_ and means just what it says, especially of malicious and unjustifiable feelings for others, whether toward the innocent or by mutual animosity.[13]

I don't know about you, but these are some of the most difficult words we have read thus far. If we hate our brother, God's Word says we still live in darkness. It's impossible to walk in fellowship with our Father in heaven if we are out of fellowship with even one of His children.

Read Matthew 5:21–26. How does Matthew's teaching relate to our discussion?

_____

_____

_____

Not only will we walk in darkness, John wrote we will stumble around in that darkness.

No direction.

No solid footing.

If you've ever found yourself in a dark room or movie theater, you get this. We bump into things and knock things over, gaining bumps and bruises along the way. And, if there are others in the room, we stumble over them and, worse, they may stumble over us. In darkness, we not only stumble ourselves, but we can cause others to stumble.

I found a great illustration on this topic:

A man who was walking down a dark street one night saw a pinpoint of light coming toward him in a faltering way. He thought perhaps the person carrying the light was ill or drunk, but as he drew nearer he could see a man with a flashlight carrying *a white cane.*

"Why would a blind man be carrying a light?" the man wondered, and then he decided to ask.

The blind man smiled. "I carry my light, not so *I* can see, but so that *others* can see me. I cannot help being blind," he said, "but I can help being a stumbling block."

Don't you love that! The best way to help other Christians not to stumble is to love them. Love makes us stepping-stones; hate makes us stumbling blocks.[14]

I love this! May we all be stepping-stones!

The only guaranteed way for us to grow deeper in our walk with God is by walking in the light. And walking in light means walking in love. If we fail to walk in love, we arrest our faith walk. We remain stagnant or, worse, go backward.

It's confession time. I'm a sports mom. And walking in love is sometimes hard in the sports arena. Years ago, when my son was in fifth grade, he played on a neighborhood recreational basketball team. To our great surprise and delight, his team made the playoffs. The game was close, really close. Tempers flared on and off the court. I watched from the stands as the coach of the opposing team berated his son from the sidelines for mistakes he made on the court. Over and over again. It disturbed my mama's heart. At one point, he pulled aside his son and continued his tirade in front of his bench and the entire gym. Fury rose in me. I could hardly contain myself. I forgot all about the score of the game, my son's performance, or anything else. I was obsessed with this coach and outraged that no one stepped in to stop his rants.

At the end of the game, quaking with anger, I marched across the court and walked right up to that coach. I initiated a tirade of my own, raising my voice to a level I rarely used. My harsh words erupted and spewed until my son's assistant coach came over, gently took me by the arm, and walked me back across the court.

As we walked to the car, my anger lingered. I couldn't stop thinking of the demeaning and shaming words that sweet boy's father spoke over him. *What was life like at home? How could a father say those things to his son?* Gut honesty here. I didn't feel a bit sorry for what I had said. I was sure my words would make him think about what he had done. No one else stood up to him. No one else defended his son. Someone had to speak up.

A few years later, our family was leaving church. I heard a man call my husband's name. We turned to see who it was, and it was that coach. My heart sank. I couldn't excuse myself fast enough. I told my husband I had to go to the ladies' room. I couldn't face that man.

Why? I was embarrassed. God did a work in my heart in the bathroom stall that day. Since that rant on the court, I had grown in my faith. I knew God's Word, and it filled my heart. I knew that I had not modeled Jesus's example that day in the gym. Love one another? That I did not. Fly off the handle? That I did. Set a godly example? That I did not. Speak out of turn? That I did.

Eight years have passed. My son now plays college basketball. The middle school, high school, and AAU teams through those years presented me with many opportunities to lose it again. Whether it be with a coach, another parent, an opposing player, or even my son. But that moment changed me. Not perfectly, mind you. I've had a few moments. But most of the time, I have remained well behaved. I've not lost it the way I did that day so many years ago. Mostly because I have a treasury of truths to speak over myself in those moments. I remember who I am and Whose I am. I am a child of God, and I represent Him everywhere I go.

I ask myself questions. "Will I walk in the light or stumble in the darkness? Will I behave in ways that lead others to the light or lead them to stumble?"

Having the love of Jesus coursing through my veins has changed me. It changes my actions and reactions. And how thankful I am for that.

John's good news comes in verse 10! Living out God's love guarantees we walk in the Light. We remain in perfect fellowship with God and others. We won't find ourselves stumbling and bumbling around, and we will rarely be a stumbling block to others.

Be encouraged, my friend. We don't walk this walk alone! God floods our hearts with His love as we spend time with Him and in His Word. And the Spirit of God empowers us to love in ways we never thought possible! His Holy Spirit takes the "old" and blends it with the "new" to create God's perfect love in us!

Apply It

Christian love is practical. It applies to our everyday lives. There is not a single day that God will not call us to practically live out His love in our daily relationships.

Look up the following verses and note how they relate to our discussion today and how you can live them out in your life.

♥ **Romans 12:10**

_____

_____

♥ **Romans 12:16**

_____

_____

♥ **Romans 14:13**

_____

_____

♥ **Galatians 6:2**

_____

_____

♥ **1 Thessalonians 5:11**

_____

_____

♥ **James 5:16**

_____

_____

Jesus's love sets the standard of love for all believers. John 13:34 says, "So I give you a new command: Love each other *deeply and fully*. Remember the ways that I have loved you, and demonstrate your love for others in those same ways" (The Voice). And He repeats that command in John 15:12: "My command is this: Love each other *as I have loved you*" (emphasis added).

So, let's not compare the way we love with the way someone else loves. Because, in our flesh, we will almost always choose someone who doesn't model God's love as defined by 1 Corinthians. Rather, let's compare our love with the love modeled by Jesus.

As we close today, search your heart. Do you harbor anything against a brother or sister in Christ or maybe a family member? Or is someone holding a grudge against you? Get honest before God. Bring this ungodly emotion (hatred, bitterness, unforgiveness) out into the light. Take one step.

Find a way to actively engage the love of Christ in this relationship. Maybe a simple prayer is all you have to offer right now. That's enough. Maybe it's a letter. Maybe a phone call. God will reward your obedience. He will bring healing and wholeness in your heart and in your relationship. Love will replace hate. Peace will replace angst. Joy will replace sadness. Hope will replace despair.

DAY FOUR

In the World but Not of the World

MEMORY VERSE: *We know that we have come to know him if we keep his commands.* (1 John 2:3)

I met her at the close of an event. She slowly walked toward me, her tear-filled eyes looking deep into mine. "I need prayer," she whispered. "I've lost everything, and it's all my fault."

I led her to a quiet place. We sat side by side, her hand in mine. "How can I pray for you?" I asked.

She was a woman who at first blush seemed to have it all . . . a loving husband, two precious children, a home in the suburbs with great girlfriends, and a part-time job she loved which allowed her to work from home. A full life.

Yet, she shared that her heart felt restless and unsettled. Something was missing. Life had become routine. Her husband traveled, leaving her home alone. Often. In those lonely nights, she began to question her husband's fidelity, her marriage, her life.

Was he having affairs? Did he really love her? Did she really love him? Shouldn't there be more to marriage than what they had? More fun? More excitement? More intimacy? More romance?

Then, she met a stranger. A man who spoke words she longed to hear. A man who seemingly valued her. A man who appeared to listen to her. A man whose attention brought excitement and adventure.

She confessed that she had settled in her heart, even put in place a plan, to leave her husband.

But God! His timing, perfect. Throughout the weekend, God met her. Shining light into darkness. Speaking truth into lies. Interrupting her secret affair. The walls she had so carefully erected crumbled around her. As only God can do, He used His living and active Word to penetrate her heart and tear down every lie the father of lies had been feeding her. The lies that her joy, her peace, her security, her beauty, her value, her happiness could be found anywhere other than Jesus.

Friend, I've come to learn that this young woman is not alone. We spend years chasing the things of this world. Things we think will complete us. Make us feel whole. Loved. Valued. Happy. Secure.

But God's Word makes clear that everything this world offers is temporary. Everything.

God created our souls to hunger for what is eternal. And *that* is why nothing in this world will ever satisfy. Ever. Only the things of God, the riches of Christ, can fully fill and satisfy this secret place. Only God can make us feel complete, loved, and secure.

John speaks to this very truth in our next passage from 1 John 2.

Read 1 John 2:12–17, focusing especially on verses 15–17.

Digging Deeper

Write 1 John 2:15 below.

_____

_____

What are we not to love?

_____

_____

What do you think John means by the phrase "the world"?

_____

_____

In the context of 1 John, "the world" speaks of the world system—its morals, values, thought processes, schemes, and activities. It derives from the Greek word *kosmos* which refers to "the present condition of human affairs, in alienation from and opposition to God."[15] The world, although created by God, is not of God.

One commentator wrote,

Kosmos (Κοσμος) refers to an ordered system. Here it is the ordered system of which Satan is the head, his fallen angels and demons are his emissaries, and the unsaved of the human race are his subjects, together with those purposes, pursuits, pleasures, practices, and places where God is not wanted. Much in this world-system is religious, cultured, refined, and intellectual. But it is anti-God and anti-Christ.[16]

First John 5:19 makes this truth very clear: "the whole world is under the control of the evil one."

Satan is the ruler of this world. I don't write this to frighten you. It's truth directly from the mouth of God. The values and attitudes that rule this world do not come from God. Rather, they are a perfect reflection of its ruler. What are these values and attitudes? First John 2:16 spells them out for us.

- ♥ The lust of the flesh (craving for physical pleasure)
- ♥ The lust of the eyes (craving for everything we see)
- ♥ The pride of life (pride in our achievements and possessions)

Satan is God's enemy. And he is *our* enemy. But remember and never forget, though Satan may be a formidable foe, he is a defeated foe! Jesus Christ defeated him on Calvary through the hammer and nails. Jesus willingly gave His life for our sins.

While Satan is aggressive, armed, and dangerous, he is not equal to Almighty God. Scripture assures us that God gave all authority in heaven and on earth to Jesus (Matthew 28:18). *All* authority. Jesus rules and reigns over Satan. For a time, though, the father of lies has temporary jurisdiction over this earth.

Without God, even at our best and strongest, we are no match for Satan. Only in the power and authority of our Three-in-One God—Father, Son, and Holy Spirit—can we overpower and overcome the schemes and deception of the evil one. It's only when we are strong in the Lord and in His mighty power, covered in His armor, that we will walk in victory (Ephesians 6:10–17)!

Love the world or love God. It's a choice. Every day, many times a day, life presents us with opportunities to choose. The choice is ours.

Loving God requires that we remain ever alert and refuse to fall prey to the world's value system.

Read Joshua 24:15, Matthew 6:24, and James 4:4. How do these verses reinforce John's teaching?

_____

_____

_____

We must put systems in place to protect against falling prey to the world. This begins with identifying the things of this world that draw us into friendship with the world rather than friendship with God.

What things of this world vie for your affection?

_____

_____

_____

Reread 1 John 2:16. Take each of the three attitudes that characterize "everything in the world" mentioned earlier and note what they represent to you. If you are currently struggling with any of these, describe your struggle and what tools you use to overcome it.

♥ The lust of the flesh: inward desires (For more on this topic, see Galatians 5:16–21; 1 Peter 2:11.)

_____

_____

_____

♥ The lust of the eyes: outward desires, what we see

_____

_____

_____

♥ Human pride: ego, self-centeredness

_____

_____

_____

Eve's temptation in the Garden of Eden and Jesus's temptation in the wilderness perfectly illustrate all three lusts. Yet, the end results of their temptation were so very different.

Eve succumbed.

Jesus overcame.

Friend, if Satan was so bold as to tempt these two sinless human beings, how much more emboldened will he be to tempt us because he knows we are fallen, weak creatures?

Know that loving the world doesn't happen overnight. It's a gradual process. And we have an enemy who is highly skilled at enticing and tempting us.

In 1 Peter 5:8, Peter warns: "*Most importantly*, be disciplined and stay on guard. Your enemy the devil is prowling around outside like a roaring lion, just waiting *and hoping for the chance* to devour someone" (The Voice). The NIV warns, "Be alert and of sober mind." Satan is very patient. He pounces at the most opportune time, when we are weak, weary, and plumb worn out.

Let's be alert, my friend, and stay on guard.

Here are a few lessons I learned when I became a bit too comfortable with the world.

Don't become "friends" with the world.

They were just catalogs. Every week our kind mailman delivered them right to our mailbox. I coveted the images on each and every shiny, superbly designed page, longing for the lovely things of this world, lingering at my favorites. But with me in law school and my husband a credit analyst at a bank, we could barely make ends meet as it was. Owning those beautiful things wasn't a reality.

Until we got some Christmas money.

Don't give in to the world.

I pulled out my beloved Pottery Barn catalog again. I found the earmarked page. There it was. That lovely sofa. Perfectly suited for our living room. We could almost afford it. We could use our Christmas money and charge the rest. And that's what we did. My heart leapt for joy as I watched the deliverymen maneuver it through the door and gently place it in the spot I had envisioned it for years. It fit perfectly. As I curled up on my new sofa, I looked around at the other furniture. It was dated. Stained. Old. I picked up the catalog again. Maybe one more piece. A coffee table. A chair. Just one more piece. I'll be out of law school soon. We can charge it now and pay for it with my first paycheck.

And we did.

Don't fall in love with the world.

It became a pattern of behavior. No longer limited to furniture. Now it was clothes. Shoes. Bags. I desired the lovely things of this world . . . the things many of my friends had. Buying them made me feel happy. Content. And most of all, like I fit in.

Friendship with material things awakened a desire which aroused a love in my heart for what I couldn't afford. And before I knew it, I conformed to the world in which I lived; that wealthy lifestyle that surrounded me and to which I had grown accustomed. As we both made more money, those things became more affordable.

Oh, friend, I have learned such a hard lesson as a child of God and as a wife. How thankful I am now for God's Word which not only tells me I'm an overcomer but also gives me the tools to overcome!

To overcome the world is to gain victory over its sinful pattern of life. So, if you ever find yourself becoming too friendly with the world, I pray these tools will help you turn around and walk away:

1. **Have faith in who you are in Christ.** God makes a great promise to you in 1 John 5:4: "for everyone born of God overcomes the world." You are a blood-bought child of the One True God. Forgiven. Redeemed. Transformed. That means you, sweet friend, are an overcomer!

2. **Claim the indwelling power of God's Spirit.** God makes you another great promise in 1 John 4:4: "You, dear children, are from God and have overcome them, because the one who is in you is greater than the one who is in the world." We receive the fruit of God's Spirit. His Spirit and the fruit it brings with it lives in each one of us. That fruit includes self-control (Galatians 5:22–23). We have the power within us to say no!

3. **Stand on the Word of God.** First John 2:14 says, "the word of God lives in you, and you have overcome the evil one." God's living and active Word penetrates to the deepest places to convict us of what is sin and what is outside God's will and plan for our lives (Hebrews 4:12). His Word can help us take captive thoughts and desires that lean toward the ways of the world and replace them with Truth and the ways of God (2 Corinthians 10:5).

4. **Take one practical step** to turn away from the darkness of this fallen world and toward the light.

For me, my practical step was no more Pottery Barn catalogs. Or any other catalog for that matter. If I didn't see it, I didn't want it! I didn't buy another piece of furniture from Pottery Barn till nearly twenty years later! And, oh, is it a pretty table. I remember the day well when we walked into the store to purchase it. This time was different. I waited until it went on sale, paid cash, and bought it to fill an outward need, not an inward desire.

As we close today, spend some time with the lyrics from one of my favorite songs from one of my favorite artists, Mandisa. She acknowledges the reality of our spiritual battle. But she reminds us we are not alone in our battle. We have a God living in us who is an overcomer and, because of that, we too are overcomers. God fights on our behalf!

WE OVERCOME BY THE BLOOD OF THE LAMB AND THE WORD OF HIS TESTIMONY!

The same Man, the Great I am
The one who overcame death
Is living inside of you
So just hold tight, fix your eyes
On the one who holds your life
There's nothing He can't do
He's telling you

You're an overcomer
Stay in the fight 'til the final round
You're not going under
'Cause God is holding you right now
You might be down for a moment
Feeling like it's hopeless
That's when He reminds you
That you're an overcomer
You're an overcomer

You're an overcomer
You're an overcomer [17]

Apply It

John warns us not to love the world. When we obey this command, we remove ourselves from its temptations. However, there is a downside. When we reject the world, it will reject us, sometimes even hate us. And this is hard, even isolating at times.

John speaks to this in his gospel.

Read John 15:18–16:4.

Jesus warned His disciples of this hatred and the persecution that accompanies it (Matthew 5:10–12; Matthew 10:16–23; Mark 9:9–13). As Jesus's ministry grew and His teachings spread, the tide of resentment, hatred, and eventually open opposition increased.

Why was Jesus so hated?

_____

_____

After Jesus's death, the hostility escalated. And that hostility continues to this day. Until the Lord returns, or until we die, we will continue to witness it, and some of us will even experience it.

Reread John 15:18–20. Who does the world hate (verse 18)?

_____

_____

Why does Jesus say the world hates His followers (verses 19–20)?

_____

_____

Trusting Jesus as our Lord and Savior elevates us into a new spiritual position. Salvation moved us "out of the world" to be "in Christ." So, although we physically live in this world, we are not *of* the world. This world is not our eternal home.

Our new position should give us a new perspective. We should see the world through a different lens . . . the lens of God's Word. The world demands conformity with the patterns of this world. God demands the opposite. He says, "Do not conform to the pattern of this world." Instead, "be transformed by the renewing of your mind" through His Word (Romans 12:2).

We are to be *in* the world but not *of* the world.

What does it look like to be "in" the world but not "of" the world for you? If you feel you still live too much "of" the world, what step or steps are you willing to take to move closer to where God wants you to be?

_____

_____

_____

_____

As we close today, I find myself challenged by my opening story. Oh, not that I have met a man. But, rather, how easy it is to be tempted away from all that is right and good in our lives. God designed our souls to be filled by Him and Him alone. And if we aren't staying closely connected to Jesus, our hearts will wander just as that young woman's did. We will feel empty, restless, discontent, as though we don't have enough.

May we never be deceived into believing we are strong enough not to be tempted by all the world has to offer. Each of us is just a few decisions away from giving in to our weaknesses, making decisions whose consequences can alter our lives and the lives of those we love, forever.

Let's make a commitment today to . . .

recognize our enemy.

realize our vulnerability.

resolve to not become friends with the world.

If you find yourself struggling with any of my three Pottery Barn lessons I shared earlier (friendship with the world, giving in to the world, in love with the world), take one practical step away from "the world" and "into the light." Write a prayer asking God to equip you and strengthen you so that you can follow through and be an overcomer!

Beware of Antichrists

MEMORY VERSE: *We know that we have come to know him if we keep his commands.* (1 John 2:3)

How are you coming with your memory verse? Think of each verse as a treasure. A valuable gold nugget tucked deep in your heart. Truth to recall when temptations, doubts, fears, and questions press in. It may be for you or for someone you love. We can have head knowledge about Scripture, but it doesn't mean much if that living and active Word never travels from our heads into our hearts.

On a scale of 1–10, where 1 is a little head knowledge of God's Word and 10 is God's living and active Word filling your heart, where would you place yourself? _____

Too much of one without the other is not a good thing. Let's pray for perfect balance. A head filled with biblical truth and a passionate heart to live out that truth.

Digging Deeper

<u>Read 1 John 2:18–27.</u>

In my NIV Bible, the author titles this section "Warning Against Antichrists."

With what words does John open verse 18?

_____

_____

John refers to it being "the last hour" (1 John 2:18). Peter uses similar language in 2 Peter 3:3, "the last days." The author of Hebrews also refers to "these last days" (Hebrews 1:2). What do these words mean? To what are the writers referring?

These phrases don't refer to a specific time or event. Rather, they refer to a season or a time. Specifically, the time between Christ's first and second comings. One commentator describes it as "a period of struggle and suffering preceding a divine victory."[18] So, like Peter and John, we too live in the "last days."

These are exciting words because they signify that the final chapter of human history as we know it is now being written! That one day soon, Jesus will return and take His rightful place on God's throne. They foreshadow the time when,

"At the name of Jesus every knee should bow, in heaven and on earth and under the earth, and every tongue acknowledge that Jesus Christ is Lord, to the glory of God the Father" (Philippians 2:10–11).

When is soon? Does Scripture give us any clues as to the date, year, or even decade?

<u>Read Matthew 24:36.</u> **What does it say?**

_____

_____

Who is the only One who will know?

No man knows. No man can know. Men have proposed and will continue to propose many ridiculous theories for when the world will end. But none are true.

John issued a strong warning about this in-between time in which we live and identified a crucial piece of evidence to confirm we are truly living in it. **What was that evidence (1 John 2:18–19)?**

Antichrist is the Greek word *antichristos*, taken from the words *christo* (Christ) and *anti* (against or in place of). The term refers to anyone who opposes Christ or puts himself in the place of Christ.[19] It's a spirit that originates with the devil and motivates, energizes, and empowers the antichrist to do Satan's work on earth.

John gives us more contrasts here, contrasting two forces working against each other.

Christ and antichrist.

Good and evil.

Truth and lies.

Christ and the devil.

One empowered by the Holy Spirit and the other by Satan.

Antichrists are the great enemies of God Jesus prophesied in Matthew 24:24, "For false messiahs and false prophets will appear and perform great signs and wonders to deceive, if possible, even the elect."

And one day there will be the final Antichrist. The man of lawlessness. Paul warned of him in 2 Thessalonians 2:8–10,

"And then the lawless one will be revealed, whom the Lord Jesus will over-throw with the breath of his mouth and destroy by the splendor of his coming.

"The coming of the lawless one will be in accordance with how Satan works. He will use all sorts of displays of power through signs and wonders that serve the lie, and all the ways that wickedness deceives those who are perishing. They perish because they refused to love the truth and so be saved."

He will be Satan's tool equipped with Satan's power. Satan will employ him to lead his final rebellion against Christ.

But in 1 John 2:18–19, John warned against antichrists who would *precede* the final Antichrist. The ones living and breathing in their midst. Specifically, the Gnostics.

These men belonged to the church—often the highly regarded, successful, persuasive, and impressive teachers. But, in time, their behavior exposed their hidden agenda.

They cleverly twisted biblical truths. They bragged about their outward appearances, accomplishments, and power. They cast doubts on the legitimate teachers in the church by spreading lies about them.

John called the Gnostics out for what they were: liars and deceivers. He repeatedly issued warnings to expose their schemes and deception to keep his children alert and on guard.

Read 1 John 2:19. Why do you think the Gnostics didn't really belong to, or connect with, the church?

_____

_____

Read 1 John 2:20. What distinguished the "true believers" from the Gnostics?

_____

_____

John speaks in verse 20 of an "anointing." In the New Testament, this word referred to one thing being applied to another for a particular purpose. When speaking of the "anointing" of the Holy Spirit, it refers to God sending His Spirit into the world to indwell the heart of every person who accepts His Son, Jesus, as their Lord and Savior (2 Corinthians 1:21–22). The moment we invite Jesus into our lives, God's Spirit takes up residence in our hearts. We are sealed with His Spirit always and forever!

Second Corinthians 1:21–22 testifies to this truth: "Now it is God who makes both us and you stand firm in Christ. He anointed us, set his seal of ownership on us, and put his Spirit in our hearts as a deposit, guaranteeing what is to come."

The indwelling presence of God's Spirit gives us the ability to not only know truth but also detect lies and recognize error.

Remember back in Week 1 when we talked about counterfeit Christians? We circle back to them today. Today's teaching shines a light on the counterfeit believers in Paul's time. The Spirit enables us to detect false teachers. Initially, their teachings seemingly align with those of the church. They use familiar church lingo. But over time, discrepancies surface. Their teachings no longer match up with God's Word, church doctrine, and the long-standing tenets of the faith.

A church that is strong in the truth will expose both the false teachings and the false teachers, causing them to lose their power and influence. Eventually, the false teachers will leave, leaving a wake of destruction behind. They often take a band of followers, dividing the church and destroying the unity and love that once bonded the fellowship. This shouldn't surprise us since one of Satan's names, *diablos*, means "the divider."

As believers, how can we recognize these false teachings and teachers?

Look for teachers who deny the deity of Christ, meaning the biblical revelation that Jesus is the Son of God.

In denying the deity of Christ, who else do false teachers reject (1 John 2:22–23)?

_____

_____

False teachers distort the Bible's teaching on who Jesus is.

Read Jude 3–14. What does Jude have to say about this in verses 3–4?

_____

_____

False teachers tweak biblical truth to suit their purposes. The Gnostics taught grace but twisted its meaning to advocate that being saved by grace meant they could sin without restraint and without consequences.

Jude's description of these false teachers in verses 12–13 creates powerful word pictures of the hearts of these men. Explain what these verses say to you about the hearts and actions of false teachers.

_____

_____

The good news. We, as children of God, need not fear being led astray by these false teachers because the One who lives in us (the Holy Spirit) is a sound interpreter of God's Word and of the hearts of the men who claim to teach His Word. He will lead us into all truth. John 16:13 says, "But when he, the Spirit of truth, comes, he will guide you into all the truth. He will not speak on his own; he will speak only what he hears, and he will tell you what is yet to come."

But knowing and recognizing false teachings is not enough. We also must be prepared to combat the lies cloaked in their tweaked versions of the truth!

John's closing words in this portion of Scripture make my heart sing as a Bible teacher and are encouraging words for all of us who study God's Word.

Write 1 John 2:27 below.

_____

_____

_____

How does this verse encourage you as you read God's Word today?

_____

_____

This Scripture does not suggest eliminating Bible teachers and pastors. We will always need gifted men and women to teach and preach God's Word . . . to lead His sheep from shallow into deep, from milk to meat.

We must read this in context of the time in which John wrote his letter, the setting in which the people lived. He wrote to challenge the Gnostics who insisted there was more to the faith than what the apostles were teaching. Who claimed there was a higher truth known only to them.

But there is only one source of Truth. The Bible. The inspired, inerrant, living Word of God (John 17:17; 2 Timothy 3:15–16; Hebrews 4:12). God's written revelation to His people never to be superseded by man's thoughts or ideas (Deuteronomy 4:2, 32; Galatians 1:6–12; 1 Corinthians 4:6; Revelation 22:18–19). It is unchangeable, final, and eternal.

Biblical truth is our standard. Anything that adds, takes away from, or twists Scripture is heretical. As children of God, we are to test everything and line it up with the Word of God, the only truth. That includes our words, actions, choices, feelings, mind, will, and emotions.

Friend, let's summarize what we have learned.

God's Word is the only Truth.

God's Truth is our standard.

We are to neither add to nor take away from God's Truth.

The Holy Spirit never reveals new truth, *ever*; He only interprets the Truth that already is.

The Spirit enables us to understand God's Truth already revealed in the Scriptures found between Genesis and Revelation.

Read John 16:13. What does it say?

_____

_____

John's words still hold relevance today. This generation proudly proclaims there are no "absolutes." What they're really saying is that truth is relative. What you think is true may be quite different from what I think is true. And that's okay. That's good because it does not offend. Without absolutes, no one has the right to claim that his or her version of truth is better than another's.

While this sounds nice in theory, think of what this looks like lived out in the real world. The men who flew jumbo jets into the World Trade Center and the Pentagon on 9/11, killing thousands of innocent people, were not terrorists; they were simply religious men following their convictions. The Syrian rebels who torture and kill Christians who refuse to convert to Islam are not cruel, cold-blooded killers; they are simply devout religious men seeking to take back their homeland. The driver who accidentally cut you off on the freeway and then slammed into your car would not be liable for the damages because you violated his road space. How could judges and juries pronounce people guilty or not guilty when there are no agreed-upon laws defining criminal conduct?

I know these are extreme examples, but without absolutes, without defining right and wrong, complete chaos would ensue.

What does Jesus say in John 14:6?

_____

_____

Jesus does not teach that He knows the truth or that He points the way to the truth.

Jesus *is* the Truth! His way is truth. His words are truth.

What does John 8:44 say?

_____

_____

Apply It

Let's not be caught off guard like Eve or the New Testament church. We know without a doubt Satan is the voice behind the lies. He knows there is a way that seems right to humanity, that makes sense in the world's economy. But in the end, Scripture tells us, that way leads to sin and death.

Jesus identified Satan as "the prince of this world" (John 12:31). Satan has a major influence in our world right now. He hates absolutes. So, is it any surprise that our world wants nothing to do with absolutes?

Satan loves darkness and hates light. He loves evil and hates good. He sets his agenda and our unbelieving world follows.

Yet, we need not fear Satan. Why?

First, we are children of the light, sons and daughters of the One True God, covered under the blood of Jesus. Because of that, we walk in the light; Satan no longer rules our hearts and minds. He tries. He tempts. He entices. He deceives. But he cannot rule us.

Second, God is sovereign. That sovereignty contains Satan. Satan cannot act outside God's sovereign power. He operates only within the boundaries God has set for him. So, for now Satan has power, and we must remain on alert for those who follow his ways, teach his lies, and advocate his deceptive practices. For those who expend their energy to thwart the plans of God.

1 John

Give some examples of relative truths in our society today.

_____

_____

What absolutes does Scripture teach that contradict those relative truths?

_____

_____

The Holy Spirit enables us to discern light from dark, good from evil, right from wrong, and truth from lies. God's indwelling Spirit is our Teacher and guides us into all truth. His Spirit rebukes, corrects, trains, leads, and most especially ministers to us in times of doubt and uncertainty. He protects us against ignorance and deception.

But this doesn't just happen. We aren't simply sealed with the Spirit and know everything we need to know. There are steps we must take.

♥ Recognize the battle.

♥ Study and memorize God's Word.

♥ Be alert.

♥ Apply His Word.

♥ Join a church.

♥ Surround yourself with a close circle of believing friends.

♥ Live out your faith boldly.

♥ Seek godly wisdom and discernment.

Finally, and most importantly, _pray always for all things_. Prayer activates and empowers each of the above steps and ensures we maintain a constant connection with Jesus.

Paul gives Timothy this sound advice: "Do your best to present yourself to God as one approved, a worker who does not need to be ashamed and who correctly handles the word of truth" (2 Timothy 2:15).

As we close today, spend some time pondering Paul's words to Timothy.

How can we present ourselves to God as "one approved"?

_____

_____

How can we ensure that we "correctly handle" the word of truth?

_____

_____

Let's close our time together in prayer.

Heavenly Father, Your Word tells us that deceivers will come, and many will succumb to their lies and cleverly devised schemes. We need You more than ever before to navigate this world, our culture, the enemy, and his lies. Holy Spirit, help us to be wise; to be alert so that we can recognize the schemes of the devil. Help us to discern lies from truth and stand firm on that truth. We ask this in Jesus's name. Amen.

Group Discussion Questions

1. Last week ended with an invitation for you to take a step of faith and apply something you learned during that week. Share what step you took and how God used it in your life and, if applicable, in the life of another. What did it feel like to take that step of obedience?

2. This week we talked about hard stuff. We talked about false teachers and antichrists and the final Antichrist.

   a. Before you started this study, what did you know about these topics and how did you feel about them?

   b. List three things the word *antichrist* describes.

   c. Now that you have studied these terms in more depth, has your understanding of them changed? If so, how?

3. What does contending for your faith look like in the world today? Is there a place in your life where you need to contend for your faith? If so, share about that place and one forward step of faith you can take.

4. I shared three key questions to ask when discerning whether a teacher is a false teacher.

   a. List the questions.

   b. When lined up with God's Word, the distinctions between a true teacher and a false teacher become very clear. What differences stood out to you?

5. Read 1 John 2:26–27.

   a. Explain in your own words what John says in this passage.

   b. How does this passage encourage you not only as you study God's

   Word but as you step out in obedience to contend for your faith?

WALK IN LOVE

PRAYER: *My Abba Father, thank You for showing me love when I didn't deserve it. When I was still steeped in sin, You sent Your Son to die for me. When I didn't deserve it, You reached down and loved me with the love that only You can give. You engraved my name on the palm of Your hand and etched my name in Your heart. Even now, when I mess up, when I throw fits, when I doubt Your plans, You patiently love me through it all. Help me to live and love like You. Your love is patient. Your love is kind. Your love is not proud. Your love is not easily angered. Your love has no limits! As I walk through this journey called life, enable me to not only grasp but deeply understand how high and wide and deep and long is Your love. Help me to live out Your love in my family, in my friendships, in my community. Father, make Your love alive in me. I ask this in the name of Jesus. Amen.*

Beloved Children of God

MEMORY VERSE: *Consider the kind of extravagant love the Father has lavished on us—He calls us children of God! It's true; we are His beloved children.* (1 John 3:1 The Voice)

A number of years ago, God placed a young bride named Kristy on my path. Chronic illness plagued her fragile body. My heart broke as she shared how her severe health issues made it highly improbable that her body could physically support another life for nine months.

We kept in touch through the years. At one point, Kristy's health improved enough that doctors told her if she ever had a chance to carry a baby, it was then. After much trying, she became pregnant. My heart leapt with joy as she shared her good news. But, it wasn't meant to be. Kristy lost her baby. Six months of life-threatening complications following her miscarriage led to a decision that she should never try it again . . . both for her life and the life of the baby.

Kristy's health issues prevented her from working full-time, but as her body healed, she longed to return to nursing. A position opened at Boston Children's Hospital. She interviewed, and they hired her. She fell in love with the job.

Still broken over not being able to conceive their own children, she and her husband decided to adopt—a process that was fraught with endless difficulties and complications.

Was God closing this door too?

It seemed as if every opened door closed in ways that defied reason.

During this same time, Kristy's church asked Kristy and her husband to pilot a mission trip to Haiti. They hesitated because if a baby came up for adoption while they were out of the country, they would lose the child. But in the end, they felt God's call to go.

What I haven't told you is that Kristy is a pediatric nurse with specialized training in oncology/hematology, particularly sickle cell anemia. During her fourth day of volunteering in a Haitian orphanage, the director pulled her aside and asked her to meet a ten-year-old child who had been diagnosed with "severe anemia that would kill her within a year or two." Kristy asked for any available medical records. But she knew the moment she laid eyes on the girl that the child had the disease.

Kristy spent hours with this sick child, holding and rocking her during agonizing bouts of pain. The girl needed constant hydration, so Kristy gave her a pink water bottle. This sweet child carried that water bottle wherever she went . . . even slept with it. She never left Kristy's side.

If she remained in Haiti, it meant certain death. But in America, with proper treatment, she had a chance to live a long life. Kristy and her husband knew they needed to bring this precious child to the U.S.

The quickest way to accomplish that was to bring her on a medical visa and then begin adoption proceedings.

Rather than close doors, God opened each and every one. The cost for the visa, flights, and initial medical treatment totaled eight thousand dollars. This desperate young couple stayed up all night drafting a letter asking friends and family for donations. Yet, before they had a chance to press send, a man from their church donated the full amount.

As if God hadn't shown off enough, the hospital at which Kristy worked, Boston Children's Hospital, officially accepted the girl as a patient . . . which was a prerequisite for the medical visa.

They waited for what seemed an eternity on the visa and passport to be processed, encountering a few roadblocks along the way. But. They persevered. They endured. They prayed. We prayed. They believed God at His Word. Finally, Kristy sent word that her husband had landed on American soil holding their precious Djenika in his arms!

God had gone before them and prepared the way.

They came to learn a precious lesson that I too have learned. Sometimes rejection is God's protection. Kristy and her husband had their plans, yet God closed those doors because He had a better plan. God had *chosen* precious Djenika for Kristy and her husband. And they *chose* to say yes.

This was not how Kristy imagined her family as a young bride. She dreamed of conceiving and raising her own baby. Then she dreamed of adopting an American baby and raising it as her own. Yet, God gave them a ten-year-old Haitian girl with sickle cell anemia. They fell in love with her is if she was their own, and they celebrated God's gracious provision and faithfulness.

God used Djenika to heal Kristy's broken heart. And He is using Kristy to bring not only physical healing but one day emotional and spiritual healing to this young Haitian girl.

It's amazing what love can do!

And that is where we land today. On God's extravagant love for His children. For you and for me.

Our memory verse for this chapter is 1 John 3:1.

Read this verse again and write it below. Take a few minutes to meditate on the verse and praise God for what it means to you.

_____

_____

Read John 1:12. How do we become children of God?

_____

_____

Soon we will dig deeply into this verse. But for now, I want you to see that, just as Kristy and her husband *chose* Djenika to be a part of their family, God has chosen *you* to be part of His family. If you have received Jesus as your Lord and Savior and believe in His Name, you are a child of the One True God. A beloved daughter of the King of Kings and Lord of Lords.

Let that soak into your heart and deep into the marrow of your bones!

Digging Deeper

I like to read various translations when I want to more deeply understand a verse or passage of Scripture. In the King James Version, our memory verse reads, "Behold, what manner of love the Father has bestowed upon us, that we should be called sons of God" (1 John 3:1). The NIV uses the word *see* rather than *behold*.

Let's dissect this verse a bit further. The Greek word translated *see* (*idete*) is both a command and an exclamation that exhorts us to give close attention to the rest of what is being spoken.[20] The rest of what is spoken in this case is "what manner of love" (King James). Or as the NIV says, "what great love." God's love is unlike any other. It is the kind of love that brings wonder and amazement. John invited his readers to open their eyes and see for themselves this amazingly great, out-of-this-world love.

Evidence of this love surrounded them, and they just needed to open the eyes of their hearts to perceive it.

God's love is a peculiar love, unlike anything in the natural world. In fact, it's impossible to contain God's love in words, but Paul describes it best for us in 1 Corinthians.

Read 1 Corinthians 13:4–8. Describe the character of God's love and how you have experienced His love in your life.

_____

_____

Choose one characteristic of God's love you'd like to refine. Commit to live it out in the next forty-eight hours, and then describe how God used your obedience.

_____

_____

How I long to grasp the true character of God's love and truly partake of that love. It seems too immense, too far out of reach for a fallen creature like me, who continually disappoints and disobeys Him. Some understand His love easier than others. Me, I have always struggled to make it deeply personal. I'm not sure why. But I know that when we comprehend deep in our souls the vast reality of God's revolutionary love . . . His unconditional, lavish, exquisite love . . . it will alter our hearts and lives forever.

How do I know this? Because of the revolutionary life-change we observe in John's life throughout the New Testament. Early in his ministry, we find a brash and ambitious young man, sometimes even arrogant. In Luke 9:46–48 and Luke 22:24, John joins in disputes with the disciples as to who among them was the greatest. Later, we find John attempting to stop a man from driving demons out in Jesus's name because he was not one of them. Jesus rebuked John for his attitude. Also in Luke 9, John asked permission to call fire down on a Samaritan village that failed to welcome Jesus and His followers. Again, Jesus rebuked him.

In Mark 10, we find the most bold and audacious of John's requests.

Read Mark 10:35–45. What did John ask?

_____

_____

Wow! Can you imagine asking Jesus to reserve a seat of honor for you? John's words exposed his burning desire for position and power. Bold and brash? Absolutely!

Oh, I wish I could say I'm not guilty of the same, but I am. There are times when I have compared myself to unbelievers or those who don't "live as godly a life as me" and asked God why . . . why do they receive blessings and I don't, or why do I suffer and they don't? Have you asked that question?

I have also asked why He chooses to honor those who fail to honor Him. It's shameful to admit these thoughts. But how thankful I am that our God is a God of mercy and grace and continues loving me despite myself!

How did Jesus reply to James and John in verses 38–40?

_____

_____

You see, friend, John had it backward in his early years. He didn't get what it meant to be chosen and called by God. He saw himself as greater than he was.

Jesus's words to John taught a concept foreign to that culture and to our culture today.

What is the revolutionary concept Jesus revealed to His disciples in verses 42–45?

_____

_____

Perhaps instead of demanding, "Teacher, we want you to do for us whatever we ask," James and John should have asked, "Teacher, what can we do for you?" I believe that over the years, as John ministered in Jesus's name, and as he suffered persecution because of Jesus's name, God opened his eyes to behold and his heart to perceive the height, depth, width, and length of God's love. And as he grew in the knowledge of that love, his heart softened and his expectations changed.

The book of 1 John wonderfully reflects that transformation. John abandoned ambition for affection. The transformed John believed in and fully received the unconditional, lavish love of Jesus. He understood it and pursued it above all else . . . above power, prestige, position, and honor.

John, in turn, became an overflowing fountain of that love. Teaching his spiritual children to know, realize, and receive that love became his burning passion.

Do you remember another man of God who began arrogant and proud? A Jew who persecuted God's people until the love of Christ invaded his heart?

Who do you think I'm talking about? (See Acts 9.)

_____

_____

Paul too knew the depth of God's love and prayed for us to know it as well in one of the most beautiful and oft-quoted prayers in Scripture.

Read Ephesians 3:17–19.

Don't you want to know this love? Experience this love? It's a love that exceeds all reason. Spans all dimensions. The _full_ measure of that love cannot be *known* this side of heaven. But, by God's grace, that love inhabits us. It's a fruit of His Spirit (Galatians 5:22) and comes alive in us when we receive Jesus as our Lord and Savior. So, we don't need to ask for it. It's ours. But we *do* need to pray for God to enable us to behold it . . . perceive it . . . experience it . . . live fully in it . . . as much as we possibly can!

Just as Djenika received the lavish love of Kristy and her husband and has been adopted into their family, we receive the lavish love of God and are adopted into His family as soon as we receive the unmerited love of Jesus in our hearts.

Read 1 John 3:2.

We celebrate that even now we have the title "children of God"! But one day we will be more. One day we will leave behind these weak, fragile bodies fraught with sickness and imperfection, and we will receive new bodies . . . glorified bodies. One day, "we shall be like him" (1 John 3:2).

What does this mean?

Read 1 Corinthians 15:49–53. How does Paul describe this transformation?

_____

_____

Let's read a few more passages to enlighten our understanding. Jot down the truth from each.

♥ **1 Corinthians 15:42–49**

_____

_____

♥ **Philippians 3:20–21**

_____

_____

💙 **Colossians 3:4**

_____

_____

💙 **1 Thessalonians 4:16–18**

_____

_____

Read these beautiful words from Romans 8:29 found in The Message paraphrase:

"God knew what he was doing from the very beginning. He decided from the outset to shape the lives of those who love him along the same lines as the life of his Son. The Son stands first in the line of humanity he restored. We see the original and intended shape of our lives there in him."

The fancy term for this transformation is glorification. Glorification follows salvation and sanctification. Salvation occurs the moment we invite Jesus into our hearts. We are saved from eternal damnation and receive the gift of eternal life. At that point, we begin a walk of sanctification. We move from "glory to glory" as we walk with God. He transforms us from the inside out as we grow closer in our relationship with Him. Second Corinthians 3:18 says it well,

"And we all, who with unveiled faces contemplate the Lord's glory, are being transformed into his image with ever-increasing glory, which comes from the Lord, who is the Spirit."

Share some of the sanctifying work God has done in your life . . .
ways you have seen Him transform you to be more like Jesus (more
patient, more kind, more loving, more peaceful, more trusting).

_____

_____

_____

_____

_____

Glorification comes at the end of our journey when God transforms our mortal physical bodies into eternal physical bodies. Imperishable, perfect in power and strength. Bodies in which we will dwell forever and ever.

Philippians 3:21 says that Jesus will "transform these humble, *earthly* bodies into the form of His glorious body" (The Voice). The word *transform* here in the Greek speaks of an outward, not an inward, change. Our inward change happens on this earth through the process of sanctification in which we grow closer and closer in Spirit with Jesus as we walk with Him day by day. But with glorification, which comes at the end of our lives, God transforms our physical bodies into the same form as Jesus's glorified body. (If you want to get a bit technical, Jesus was the first resurrected from the dead in a glorified body, thus God called Him the first fruits of creation [1 Corinthians 15:20]. And His resurrection is the promise and guarantee of the resurrection of all believers.)

The bottom line is that glorification clothes us with the very same glory that clothes Jesus! God's glory enswathing us! Hallelujah! Can you even imagine?

In our earthly state, we cannot even look upon God's glory. Remember when Moses asked God to show him His glory? God responded to Moses that he could not look upon God's face because no man could see God and live! So, He hid Moses in the cleft of a rock to protect him. God then covered Moses with His hand and allowed His glory to pass by. After

He passed by, God removed His hand and allowed Moses to see His back (Exodus 33:12–23).

As sinful, fallen creatures, we cannot look upon God's glory. But on that glorious glorification day, gazing through our newly glorified eyes, John announces in verse 2 that we will see Jesus as He really is . . . in all His glory! We will lay eyes upon our Lord and Savior and see Him for the very first time!

A natural question that follows this incredible news: *what will our resurrected bodies be like?* Of course, we truly won't know until we receive such a body ourselves, but we gain insight from the Scriptures.

Read Mark 16:14; Luke 24:30–31; and John 20:26–28. What do you learn about Jesus's resurrected body? Think a bit outside the box. What insight do these passages give about how the resurrected body differs from ours (how it works and runs) and what it looks and feels like?

It seems Jesus's body moved through closed doors, yet He could eat and digest food. In John 20, Jesus invited Thomas to touch His nail-scarred hands and put his hands *into* Jesus's side, so clearly His body was solid enough to retain scars and be touched. From these accounts, Jesus's body defied the laws of nature.

Take a minute to "dream" about your resurrection body. What are you most looking forward to?

Apply It

Don't you wonder what our lives would be like if we truly lived in the absolute assurance of God's love? Yes, we may *know* in our heads that God loves us. We quote verses, sing worship songs, hang framed pictures, hold signs at football games, and sport stickers on our car windows speaking of this love.

But John desires not just that we *know* God's love but that we *live* loved. That we live as if we really believe it down to the marrow of our bones. God longs for us to walk confidently in the certainty of His love even when our emotions, feelings, and circumstances cry otherwise.

My prayer is that we begin a new thought process together. A process whereby we train our hearts and minds to live loved . . . to evaluate everything through the filter of God's eternal, unchanging, magnificent, exquisite love. No ifs, ands, or buts about it.

Are you up for this? Will you join me? No matter the words someone speaks about you or to you. No matter the fact you were left off an invitation list. No matter the diagnosis you receive after an MRI. No matter the anxiety that plagues your heart each day. No matter the child who comes in the door with 3 Ds on her report card. No matter the husband who says he needs time apart. No matter the shame Satan tries to heap on you. No matter ANYTHING. Let's agree together as daughters of the One True God to process everything that crosses our path, not through our broken and hurting hearts, but through the lavish love of God that is ours in Christ Jesus.

What is one circumstance going on in your life that you need to filter through God's love for you? As you bring that before the Lord, pray this prayer from Isaiah 54:10:

Heavenly Father, though the mountains be shaken and the hills be removed, Your unfailing love for me will not be shaken. Help me to trust You with _____ *and see it as a way to plumb the depths of Your love and fully surrender my heart to You and depend on You and You alone. I ask this in Jesus's name. Amen.*

DAY TWO

Sin

> **MEMORY VERSE:** *Consider the kind of extravagant love the Father has lavished on us—He calls us children of God! It's true; we are His beloved children.* (1 John 3:1 The Voice)

S IN.

What's the first thing that pops into your mind when you see this three-letter word?

It's a word many of us avoid talking about or even thinking about. I did for a long time. But it's a recurring word and theme in Scripture. God has much to say about it. And if God has much to say about it, we best pay attention to it.

Before we dig in to John's teaching on sin, let's engage in a little word study. You know I'm a word nerd and love to take us back to original languages. First, let's clarify the kind of sin we are talking about. John speaks of "sin," singular; not "sins," plural.

What's the difference? Sin is the power that reigns over us and moves us to commit sins, plural. Adam and Eve's tragic choice downloaded the propensity to sin into every generation of human beings.

Sins are the fruit of sin. They are the specific sinful acts in which we engage. Pride. Jealousy. Lying. Cheating. Gossiping. Stealing. Idolatry. Rage. You get the idea.

Digging Deeper

Read 1 John 3:4–10.

Sin, as used in verse 4, derives from the Greek word *hamartia*; it means "missing the mark."[21] It's an archer's term and denotes more than just missing the target now and again. Oftentimes, in an archery competition, missing the target completely disqualifies the archer, meaning no second chances.

In our Christian faith, we sin—we miss the mark—each time we break God's commands. Without Christ in our lives, we are incapable of ever measuring up to God's moral standard on our own. Consequently, we will miss the mark every time. Scripture clearly states that *all* have sinned and fall short of the glory of God (Romans 3:23).

In 1 John 3:4, the King James Version defines sin as a "transgression" of God's law. Another Greek word used for sin is *anomia*, which means "lawlessness, wickedness, inequity." It is a willful, flagrant violation of God's law.[22] The NASB says sin is "lawlessness."

Read 1 John 3:4 in your Bible and write what it says below. What words does your translation use?

_____

_____

The bottom line: sin is that which is contrary to God. Jesus prophesied in Matthew 24:12 that an increase of lawlessness will mark the end times. We need only turn on the morning news or read the newspaper to confirm this truth.

But don't despair! We find good news amid all this talk of sin, my friend!

Read 1 John 3:5.

First John 3:5 brings the good news. God sent Jesus to pay the penalty for our sin. Jesus not only died for our sin, He forgave our sin once and for all! The lawlessness that once marked a believer's life has been removed as far as the east is from the west (Psalm 103:12). Isaiah the prophet wrote, "Come on now, let's walk and talk; let's work this out. Your wrong-doings are blood-red, but they can turn as white as snow. Your sins are red like crimson, but they can be *made clean again* like *new* wool" (Isaiah 1:18 The Voice).

Jesus, the sinless Lamb of God, was the only One who could free us from our sin. And He did just that on the cross at Calvary.

Celebrate this great news with me!

Take a few moments to thank Jesus for His amazing grace. Thank Him that by His crimson blood shed on the old rugged cross, the old has gone and the new has come (2 Corinthians 5:17). We are all new creations!

Read 1 John 3:6 for even more good news for believers. What does the first part of this verse say?

Take a moment to digest the significance of what we've just learned. When we become a beloved child of God, a blood-bought child of the One True God, born again by faith in Jesus Christ, we cannot practice lawlessness. First John 3:6 says, "No one who lives in him keeps on sinning."

John explains the effect of sin. A person who practices sin practices lawlessness. When John speaks of sin here, he speaks of an *attitude* of the heart. He speaks of one who has a defiant and rebellious heart . . . a heart that *habitually* practices sin. It's not an occasional sinful act; it's a lifestyle of sin with no repentance for how one is living.

Why is this distinction so important? In the Old Testament, the Israelites were bound by God's law, and God judged them by their obedience or disobedience under the law. Jesus came to set us free from bondage to the law. Jesus came to pay the penalty for our disobedience, our sin.

Let's bring this down to the basics. We are born with a sin nature. We are spiritually lost. Romans 3:10–12 spells out this reality: "There is no one righteous, not even one; there is no one who understands; there is no one who seeks God. All have turned away, they have together become worthless; there is no one who does good, not even one."

Hard words to read, but we must understand and accept this truth. We are not made right with God simply because we give to the poor, attend worship services, serve in our community, and engage in religious activities. God's Word is clear: No matter how "good" we are, without Jesus as our Lord and Savior, eternal life is beyond our reach. Jesus died to fully pay the cost of our sin, and His life is the only acceptable reckoning for that sin.

Our culture bristles at this teaching, advocating there are multiple paths to God. Sadly, we find this insidious form of religious pluralism creeping into our churches today. But we, as women of God, women who daily walk in His Word, must understand that Jesus's words are very clear.

Read John 14:6. Write it below. What does it say?

_____

_____

Read Acts 4:12. What does it say?

_____

_____

Friend, we have an unpopular message. A message God calls us to proclaim and proclaim boldly. Yet it is "good news" (Mark 1:14). And not only is it good news, it's the best news, the best gift, we could ever give someone. People need to hear the message of the cross because it not only saves them from eternal separation from God but also gives them new life . . . a life filled with unconditional love, hope, joy, peace, and purpose.

Read 1 John 3:6–8.

How do we keep from missing the mark? John tells us the key is abiding in Christ, spending time with Jesus in prayer and in His Word. There isn't a magic formula. It's a process. The more time we spend with Jesus, the less we sin. It's in that quiet abiding that God humbles our hearts and trains our ears. He speaks to us and gives us ears to hear.

Abiding hinders sin's ability to have dominion over us because it pacifies the rebellious spirit and promotes a submissive spirit. Romans 8:37 promises that in Christ we are *more* than conquerors. The more we know about and walk with Jesus, the more victory abounds!

Meeting regularly with our Savior shifts our hearts away from deliberate disobedience and toward willing obedience.

Reread 1 John 3:7–8. Explain John's distinction (the differences) between "one who does what is right" and "one who does what is sinful."

_____

_____

_____

At the very core of John's message is the fact that he believes in the reality of the devil and that this devil (Satan) opposes Christ and God's people. Satan's nature differs from God's and Christ's in many ways.

♥ God is eternal; He has always existed. Satan is not; he is a created being.

♥ Christ is obedient; He was obedient unto death (Philippians 2:8). Satan is a rebel, a murderer from the beginning.

♥ God is omnipotent (all-powerful), omniscient (all-knowing), and omnipresent (everywhere always). In the words of my pastor, Satan is omni-nothing! He is not all-powerful, not all-knowing, and not every-where always.

But the fact that a legion of fallen angels (demons) accompany Satan allows him to wreak havoc in many places at one time. Yet we need not fear Satan because of John's words in 1 John 3:8.

What does John say about Christ's role here? What does this mean for you personally?

_____

_____

Take comfort, my friend. Satan is a DEFEATED foe! And although he is certainly still at work today, Christ came to *destroy* his works. *Destroy* here means "to loose, unbind, dissolve."[23] One commentator writes, "to render inoperative, to rob of power."[24] God has crippled Satan's power and diminished his weaponry. Even better, God has outfitted us, His children, with armor and weapons of warfare to battle against the evil one. So, although he is still a mighty foe, Satan is no match for our God . . . the King of Kings, the Lord of Lords, the Commander of Heaven's Armies, the Ruler of Heaven and Earth, the Great I Am . . . and no match for the children of God!

Apply It

Read 1 John 3:9–10. Explain what John means in verse 9 when he says that no one born of God practices sin "because God's seed remains in them"? What is the "seed"?

_____

_____

_____

Within each of us lie weaknesses. Temptations with which we struggle. And it's these weaknesses that give the devil a foothold in our lives.

We must continually be on the alert for and intentionally address those temptations and lures from the devil.

Key to this process is the ability to recognize our weaknesses and temptations. If we can't recognize them, we certainly can't address them. I don't know about you, but oftentimes that's hard for me. Especially when I can justify my sin.

For years, I led a Bible study at my church. Throughout those years, I worked with various leadership teams. While at a party one night, I observed one of our leaders engaging in behavior that shocked me. My stomach churned in a mix of grief and anger. Her blatant disobedience to what I knew she knew was wrong left me frustrated and honestly, angry.

Righteous anger. The kind that God allows. Right? Have you ever experienced it? That justifiable anger that arises within you when you know someone is not acting the way they should. That anger Jesus expressed when He walked into the temple and found the moneychangers doing their business in God's house, defiling its holy ground.

Righteous anger is a good thing. However, what we do with that is another matter.

Rather than going directly to the leader, I shared my feelings about her behavior with a few other leaders while at dinner one night. Was I gossiping? In the moment, I didn't think so. In fact, I felt justified since the person about whom I was talking held a leadership position in our study and had engaged in illegal, ungodly behavior that not only reflected badly on her but on our Bible study and our church.

Our dinner conversation validated my feelings. I took comfort in how good it felt that I was not alone.

However, the next day, as I sat in church, God spoke directly to my "righteous" anger through the sermon. Our pastor spoke about idle gossip, character assassination, and how our words matter. Each word penetrated my heart like a double-edged sword.

I too was a spiritual leader. And I had flagrantly disobeyed God's Word as I judged another believer in the presence of others. Righteous anger? No. Idle gossip? Yes. Character assassination? Sadly, yes.

In the quietness of that moment, I felt conviction.

Not guilt. Not shame. But conviction.

The difference between these emotions is that guilt and shame are self-focused and unproductive. They leave us stagnant, in a bad place with God and others.

Conviction, on the other hand, is God-focused and productive. It's spurred by the Holy Spirit to point out our sin, speak truth into our hearts, and empower us to change so we live in a way that's pleasing to Him.

That day in worship, God reminded me of a truth that I have now committed to memory.

"Do not let any unwholesome talk come out of your mouths, but only what is helpful for building others up according to their needs, that it may benefit those who listen" (Ephesians 4:29).

I promised the Lord that morning, *I will hold my tongue. I will only speak words that will build others up and benefit those listening. Or, at least, I will try.*

As children of God, what steps can we take to find victory over sin? List at least three steps.

_____

_____

_____

_____

Friend, born-again children of God cannot "practice" sin, because in Christ, we receive a new nature. We no longer live governed by a sin nature. When God seals us with His Holy Spirit, a tremendous spiritual change takes place. We receive Christ's nature, His righteousness, His goodness. Christ rules and reigns in us through this new nature.

Read 1 Peter 1:23. How do Peter's words relate to John's words in 1 John 3:9?

_____

_____

In our new birth, we receive the Spirit of God. And the Spirit of God then comes alongside the Word of God to teach us about sin, convict us of sin, and empower us to repent from and turn away from sin. To make it as easy as pie, just as physical children bear the nature of their parents, spiritual children bear the nature of their Creator. We received our "old" nature from our physical birth, and we receive our "new" nature from our spiritual birth. They will battle one another. And only one will win out.

God calls us to live in alignment with our new nature, and it's our responsibility to do just that. When the new nature leads us, it leads us into a holy life. The following story brings this principle alive:

A Sunday School teacher was explaining the Christian's two natures—the old and the new—to a class of teenagers.

"Our old nature came from Adam," he explained, "and our new nature comes from Christ, who is called 'the Last Adam.'" He had the class read 1 Corinthians 15:45: "So also it is written, 'The first man, Adam, became a living soul. The Last Adam became a life-giving spirit'" (NASB).

"This means there are two 'Adams' living in me," said one of the teenagers.

"That's right," the teacher replied. "And what is the practical value of this truth?"

The class was silent for a moment, and then a student spoke up.

"This idea of the 'two Adams' really helps me in fighting temptation," he said. "When temptation comes knocking at my door, if I send the first Adam to answer, I'll sin. But if I send the Last Adam, I'll get victory."[25]

Glory! How this story speaks to my heart!

1 John

What does it look like in your life to "send the Last Adam" to face whatever hard thing you are facing?

_____

_____

_____

_____

John announced not just good news but great news! The moment we invite Christ into our hearts, we are "born of God." God's Holy Spirit takes up residence in us. This being "born again," which often carries negative connotations, is the best thing that could ever happen to us! It is more than a fresh start or a new beginning. It's a rebirth. The old is gone and the new has come. We receive a new nature, a new heart, a new name, and a new lineage.

The more we expose our hearts to God's heart and His Word, the more He renews our minds. Our renewed minds view the world through an entirely new lens. That new perspective leads to life transformation. We begin to think and act differently. The inward changes eventually translate into outward changes. Our transformed hearts lead us to speak and behave in completely new ways that will honor and glorify God.

John wrote these words with the expectation that we would not just read them but apply them. So, let's do a bit of self-examination as we close. Read through each of these questions, take them before the Lord, and answer them honestly. Choose one to spend time on this week.

1. **Am I a child of God? Have I genuinely surrendered my life to Jesus so that I know I'm forgiven of my sin and His Spirit lives in me?** If you haven't, take a step toward that today. Talk about it with a friend or a pastor. Study more about what you have learned. Or maybe you are ready to take the marvelous step of faith and invite Christ into your life with this simple prayer: *Dear Jesus, I know that I'm a sinner. I ask for Your forgiveness. I believe You died on the cross just for me*

and for my sins and that You rose from the dead so that I could have eternal life. I turn from my sins and toward You. Today I not only confess my sins, but I turn away from them and turn completely to You. Come into my heart, Jesus. I want to trust and follow You as my Lord and my Savior. Help me to live in my new nature. Transform my heart and mind to be more like You. I ask this in Your name. Amen.

2. **Do I spend time with Jesus (abiding in Him), reading my Bible and praying, to cultivate and strengthen my new nature?** If not, what step(s) can you take today to begin abiding more?

3. **Do I harbor unconfessed sin or easily fall into temptation?** If yes, take a step(s) to confess that sin or flee from that temptation and execute a plan to not return to it.

4. **Does my "old" nature rule over me more than my "new" nature?** If so, prayerfully consider why and ask the Lord to help you take a step(s) toward changing that balance of power.

As you take these steps, claim these promises from God:

"I can do all this through him who gives me strength." (see Philippians 4:13)

"In whatever I am facing, I am more than a conqueror through Jesus who loves and died for me." (see Romans 8:37)

"I am a new creation in Christ. Today I believe and walk in this truth: the old me has gone and the new me has arrived!" (see 2 Corinthians 5:17)

The Mark of a Christian

MEMORY VERSE: *Consider the kind of extravagant love the Father has lavished on us—He calls us children of God! It's true; we are His* beloved *children.* (1 John 3:1 The Voice)

From the beginning, God has called His people to love Him and to love each other. Leviticus 19:18 states clearly, "Do not seek revenge or bear a grudge against anyone among your people, but love your neighbor as yourself. I am the LORD." *The Dictionary of New Testament Theology* comments, "Love in this context means devotion toward one's neighbor for his sake, accepting him as a brother and letting him come into his own." [26]

Jesus carried God's message to love into the New Testament, both in the life He lived and the life He gave. Jesus, in the shadow of the cross, demonstrated the greatest act of love. In so doing, He prepared His disciples for what was to come. Jesus exemplified what the Father and Son desired to be the distinguishing mark of His followers . . . of all believers in Jesus.

Read John 13:33–35. What is that distinguishing mark?

_____

_____

Digging Deeper

John continues to teach using contrasts. We encounter another one here. In 1 John 1, John contrasted light and darkness. In this chapter, he contrasts love and hate.

Let's take a step back in time and visit an Old Testament family who had some serious family drama going on.

Read 1 John 3:10–16 and Genesis 4:1–10.

Who was John speaking to in this section of his letter (1 John 3:11)?

_____

_____

John directed his words to believers . . . to us. The "you" referred to people who knew, loved, and had given their lives to Jesus.

Interestingly, before he defined what love was for his audience, he defined what love was *not* through the story of Cain and Abel and their sibling rivalry.

Who were Cain and Abel, and what were their respective occupations (Genesis 4:1–2)?

_____

_____

What offering did each bring to the Lord (verses 3–4)?

How did God respond (verses 4–5; see also Matthew 23:35; Hebrews 11:4)?

Why do you think God reacted differently to their offerings?

What was Cain's immediate response to God's disapproval (verse 5)?

Why do you think God disapproved of Cain's offering (verses 6–7)?

God does not explicitly state in this passage why He refused Cain's offering. Did Cain not give the type of sacrifice he knew God required? Did he not give the best of what God asked? Did Cain offer it with an improper attitude?

It's such a difficult story, but even here, we witness God's amazing grace.

Prayerfully reread and examine God's words to Cain in verses 6–7. About what did God warn him? What do these verses teach us about Cain's heart and God's heart?

We can presume God's words to Cain fell on deaf ears because of what transpired next.

Cain chose not to listen to God's words. Instead, he listened to the voice of the evil one . . . the one whose mission it is to deceive and lead us into disobedience.

Let's dig a bit deeper.

Read Genesis 4:8.

Here we encounter the first shedding of innocent blood in the Bible. Cain murdered his brother.

John uses strong language when speaking of Cain. He says Cain "belonged" to the evil one (1 John 3:12). These words denote an aggressive, fervent evil that actively opposes what is good.[27] Cain intentionally chose to do that which was evil. John gives further insight into Cain's heart when he tells us that he "murdered" his brother. The King James says he "slew" his brother. The verb used is specific and means "to butcher or slaughter . . . and implies a violent death."[28] The bottom line: Cain slit his brother's throat.

What drove Cain to take his brother's life?

_____

_____

Read John 8:44. Who else is a murderer?

_____

_____

Times have not changed. We find intense hatred of goodness and righteousness all around us today. Almost daily we hear stories of Christians around the world being persecuted, kidnapped, harassed, tortured, even murdered.

Sometimes it's a believer's bold stance against evil that draws such persecution. But based on John's words in 3:12, it may also be a believer's unyielding faith, kindness, and/or goodness that arouses feelings of guilt and inadequacy in the unbeliever. The light shining from within one exposes the darkness—unrighteous deeds, false beliefs, lies, wickedness— in the other.

What does John say in 1 John 3:13? Does this remind you of another man in the Bible? (Hint: He built an ark.) How did the "world" respond to Noah's heart of goodness and obedience (see Genesis 6–7)?

_____

_____

Cain's actions appall us. But if I'm honest, I experience similar emotions. Maybe you do too. Hurts, jealousies, frustrations build up like a volcano just waiting to blow. They may not lead us to bloodshed, but they do result in unholy conduct or hurtful, even hateful, words.

Jesus makes it abundantly clear, hatred is the moral equivalent of murder (Matthew 5:21–22). It isn't only our outward actions that God cares about. He cares about our hearts. When we harbor hatred in our hearts, it infects our hearts with sin. Sin that takes root and goes deep. Sin is sin in the eyes of God. It all leads us to darkness, separating us from intimacy with Him. We can't hear His voice or receive His discipline. When we don't walk in the light and love about which John has been teaching, we will fall prey to the very same emotions that spewed from Cain.

Where is our hope? In our Abba Father. Our Creator. The One True God.

God is love (1 John 4:16). It is _who_ He is. It is His nature, and that nature will never change (Hebrews 13:8). Miraculously, that very same love lives in us when we receive Jesus as our Lord and Savior, because God plants His love in our hearts. By the power of God's Holy Spirit living in us, God's love has the capacity to reign and rule our hearts.

Notice I said "has the capacity" to reign and rule our hearts. There is a choice involved here. We have a choice regarding who or what reigns supreme in our hearts. God's love lives and abides in us and most assuredly changes our relationship with Him. It's walking in the fullness of that love that has the capacity to change our relationships with other people. Even the ones we find most difficult to love.

Although God is perfect and His love is a perfect love, we are not perfect. Sin taints our love. So even when we surrender our hearts and pray for God's love to reign and rule in our hearts, we may still experience occasional incidents of anger and outbursts of temper. But such behavior is not the norm. It is not our usual practice. God will patiently work with us.

What God abhors are intentional, habitual acts of anger and hatred. This deeply rooted, all-consuming hatred is what leads to death and eternal separation from God (1 John 3:14–15).

Have you noticed? With God, everything comes back to our hearts. Outward obedience is not enough. God desires sacrificial loving and giving. He asks that we give up one thing for the sake of receiving something even greater. He wants our whole heart.

God knew Cain's heart. He saw seething hatred. He saw evil. He saw jealousy. He saw pride.

Don't miss the warning tucked in this story. Guard your heart. Hatred and bitterness, when allowed to fester, consume our hearts like a cancer. They leave no room for Christ to abide and make Himself at home in our hearts. The author of Hebrews addresses this warning head-on.

What does Hebrews 12:15 say? How does a root of bitterness take root?

Take a few minutes to sit with this verse. Prayerfully ask the Lord to reveal any bitterness (even a smidgen) that has taken or is attempting to take root in your heart. Identify it. Humble yourself before

the Lord and confess it. Ask Him to help you heal the hurt that is ultimately fueling your bitterness.

_____

_____

_____

Friend, Jesus is the answer. Jesus's abiding presence empowers us to no longer live driven by our flesh, like Cain. He enables us to *choose* to allow God's Spirit to reign and rule in our hearts so we have the capacity to live a life of deep and abiding love.

John commands his audience, "Do not be like Cain." Then he goes on to explain *why* Cain acted as he did: "Because his life was devoted to evil *and selfishness*, and his brother chose to do what is right" (1 John 3:12 The Voice).

When God tried to draw Cain back to Himself, Cain's pride prevented it. His hardened heart refused God's extension of mercy and grace. He refused the opportunity to repent and receive forgiveness.

Apply It

Cain and Abel's story ended so tragically. Both boys were raised by parents who loved and worshiped God. But for this lesson, that fact didn't matter.

God does not judge us by the faith we inherit. He judges by the faith we live. With God, it's a matter of the heart. Abel loved God and did what was right in the sight of the Lord; Cain did not. He masqueraded as a true worshiper of God, but in reality, he lived for himself, not God. The selfishness and evil consuming his heart left no room for God. And when confronted with his sin, Cain could not humble his heart before God or his brother, further proving his heart was far from God.

I find it fascinating that although the Scriptures do not contain one word uttered by Abel, his exemplary faith speaks volumes, leaving an indelible example for us all to follow (Hebrews 11:4). Cain spoke many words and engaged in horrific actions that revealed no faith. God makes clear when we don't choose the way of faith, when we choose to separate ourselves from God, He will swiftly execute His judgments.

Cain's attitude symbolizes our world's attitude. Jesus warns of this attitude in John 15:18–25. John 15:19 says, "If you belonged to the world, it would love you as its own. As it is, you do not belong to the world, but I have chosen you out of the world. That is why the world hates you."

When the world, like Cain, comes face-to-face with the reality of the One True God, His love, and His truth, it can make only one of two decisions: repent and change, or attempt to destroy the One who is exposing that truth.

God calls us to live a life of love, not hate. Abel offered God his best as an act of worship. Through it, he exemplified his faith and love for God.

We can do the same. Offer God our best by living a life of love. Sometimes doing so seems hard. But, guess what? Living a life of love can be amazingly practical.

Here are a few ways we can live out our faith and offer God our best today.

♥ Sacrificially give to a stranger in need.

♥ Pray for someone who has hurt you.

♥ Extend forgiveness to a person who may not, in your mind, "deserve" your forgiveness.

♥ Accept an offer of forgiveness even though your heart struggles to do so.

♥ Offer your very best at work even if your boss is contrary and unappreciative.

Pray over this list. Invite God into the process. Ask the Lord to show you who needs to experience His love and your love. Watch and listen with anticipation for an opportunity to obey. You will stand amazed at God's handiwork. Share what happens.

DAY FOUR

Putting Feet to Living Love

MEMORY VERSE: *Consider the kind of extravagant love the Father has lavished on us—He calls us children of God! It's true; we are His* beloved *children.* (1 John 3:1 The Voice)

God calls us to love.

Well, He doesn't just call us to love; He *commands* us to love:

"You shall love the LORD your God with all your heart and with all your soul and with all your might" (Deuteronomy 6:5 NASB).

"So I give you a new command: Love each other deeply and fully. Remember the ways that I have loved you, and demonstrate your love for others in those same ways. Everyone will know you as My followers if you demonstrate your love to others" (John 13:34–35 The Voice).

We have heard these words. We know these words. We speak these words. But do we *live* these words?

John speaks of true love in this passage. His lesson in a nutshell: true love manifests itself in action. To see love in action come alive, we will visit a beloved and well-known parable. Before we begin, let's read more of John's words on love.

Digging Deeper

Read 1 John 3:16–18 and write verse 16 below.

_____

_____

John has shared his thoughts on love in previous chapters. Now John goes beyond defining love. He captures the *kind* of love God requires in 1 John 3:16, "This is how we know what love is."

To whom does John point as the ultimate example of love?

_____

_____

To what act does John point? What famous verse speaks of this act of love? (Hint: It's another 3:16 verse.)

_____

_____

Love is not passive. Real love is action. Jesus set the bar high. It's the cross—the ultimate symbol of love.

Jesus left the splendor of heaven and entered the squalor of earth for one purpose and one purpose only. For a great exchange. To give His life for ours.

Our Savior loved us so much that He willingly agreed to suffer and die on the cross for our sin. Jesus willingly obeyed His Father, came to earth, and took upon Himself the sin of the world. And that sin, sweet friend, includes your sin and mine. His sacrifice wiped our slates clean. He paid our debt *in full*. His selfless act removed the crimson stain of sin and washed us white as snow.

Take a few moments to read and meditate on the lyrics from an old hymn that says it all:

> I hear the Savior say,
> "Thy strength indeed is small;
> Child of weakness, watch and pray,
> Find in Me thine all in all."

> *Refrain:*

> Jesus paid it all,
> All to Him I owe;
> Sin had left a crimson stain,
> He washed it white as snow.

> For nothing good have I
> Whereby Thy grace to claim;
> I'll wash my garments white
> In the blood of Calv'ry's Lamb.

> And now complete in Him,
> My robe, His righteousness,
> Close sheltered 'neath His side,
> I am divinely blest.

> Lord, now indeed I find
> Thy pow'r, and Thine alone,
> Can change the leper's spots
> And melt the heart of stone.

> When from my dying bed
> My ransomed soul shall rise,

"Jesus died my soul to save,"
Shall rend the vaulted skies.

And when before the throne
I stand in Him complete,
I'll lay my trophies down,
All down at Jesus' feet. [29]

This is the gospel message. Love found its way to a cross. In the cross, we see love. We receive love. We experience love.

Jesus's selfless act taught us love is an action, not a feeling. I'll be honest, I've always thought of love as a feeling. It's how I feel about my husband and my children. It's what we feel for our parents, grandparents, brothers, and sisters. It's an emotion. But Jesus's act on the cross says it's so much more than a feeling.

Yes, feelings play a part. But they are not the entire picture. True love produces something greater than feelings. It breeds selfless, sacrificial giving. It requires humble obedience. God's love alone was not enough to redeem His children. It required a sacrifice.

The battle for our souls came to a crescendo on Calvary's hill. Our bold and brave Savior finished the war declared on God's creation in the Garden of Eden. Jesus destroyed all that stood in His path . . . and our path . . . for salvation. But the cost was tremendous: lashings, thorns, spikes, blood, tears, humiliation, cries of a mother's anguish, unimaginable pain and suffering, and finally death.

Jesus did not just talk about love; He demonstrated it.

The greatest act of love is giving one's life for another. It's love in action. But what does that look like, practically speaking, for you and me?

Let's travel back to the Gospel of Luke to learn what Jesus says about "love in action."

Read Luke 10:25–35.

Here we find Jesus engaged in a discussion with a lawyer (scribe), an expert in the Mosaic (Old Testament) Law. Not the kind of courtroom lawyer we think of today. The scribe asked Jesus a question that provided Jesus the opportunity to define relationships. He asked not out of curiosity or a true desire to know, but to test Jesus. The King James translation says the lawyer "tempted" Jesus.

Reread Luke 10:26–27. How did Jesus answer? With what did the man respond?

_____

_____

_____

Jesus answered the lawyer's question with what is known as the Socratic method. A method with which law school made me very familiar. He answered the lawyer's question with more questions. In so doing, he pointed the man to the Old Testament law. The lawyer answered as Jesus directed, with Scripture (Deuteronomy 6:5; Leviticus 19:18).

Jesus announced that the lawyer answered correctly! As a faithful Jewish scribe, he probably had memorized that verse many years earlier. He correctly understood "the letter of the law" . . . to love God and love his neighbor.

Read Luke 10:28. After Jesus told the man he answered correctly, what did Jesus say?

_____

_____

Jesus's follow-up answer probably took the man aback. It wasn't enough to know the laws; we must follow them. We must live them out. Practice what we preach.

The lawyer, knowing how tough living out the letter of the law would be, tried to limit its parameters. He asked for clarification. Who exactly was he supposed to love?

He specifically asked Jesus to define *neighbor*. Surely, it doesn't mean to love the dirty, the lame, the sick, the leper, the criminal, the drug addict, the thief.

And surely not a Samaritan.

Jesus answered the lawyer's question with a story that revealed a revolutionary truth. He spoke of a man traveling from Jerusalem to Jericho on a road known to be treacherous and dangerous, descending approximately three thousand feet in about seventeen miles. Robbers often hid along its steep, winding way, lying in wait for their next victim.[30] True to its reputation, a band of robbers stripped and beat the man (believed to be a Jew) and left him to die.

Reread the parable. As you study, I invite you to compare each character: who they were as well as their actions.

Summarize the three characters who encountered the man on the road to Jericho.

_____

_____

_____

Who passed by the injured man? Why do you think they didn't stop to help?

_____

_____

Who did Jesus cast as the hero in story? Why do you think Jesus chose him?

_____

_____

_____

How did the hero respond when he passed by the man?

_____

_____

The first two men who passed by were religious men, right? A priest and a Levite. They were Jews. Men who knew God's command to love in Deuteronomy and Leviticus. Remember too, this man on the road was a Jew. He was one of them. Yet they neither stopped nor showed compassion for him.

What were these men missing by just knowing the letter of the law?

_____

_____

Jesus ends this parable with a powerful lesson for the lawyer and for us. He chose the most unlikely person, a Samaritan, to reach out in love to the injured man. Why was this man the least likely to intervene? Jews hated the Samaritans and treated them with reproach. They were a mixed-race people produced when Jews intermarried with Gentiles. Jews detested the mixed-race people and their pagan history. They considered them garbage, not worth their time or attention.

Despite the victim's race or this racial divide, the Samaritan took compassion on him, an unexpected and unthinkable act in that culture. He could have easily passed by, and no one would have known. No one would have seen. But something deep within him—Jesus calls it compassion—moved his heart to express his love through action.

How did the Samaritan extend love (verses 34–35)?

_____

_____

Jesus knew the lawyer's heart and his prejudices. He knew the lawyer would see the Samaritan as the person least likely to act in accordance with Jewish law. Jesus knew His story would speak a hard truth into the heart of this young man's "legalistic" mind.

When Jesus asked the lawyer which of the men in His parable proved to be the injured man's neighbor, how did the lawyer respond (verse 36)?

_____

_____

Don't you find it interesting that the lawyer could not bring himself to use the word *Samaritan*? Instead, he described the man's act of mercy.

Jesus then told the lawyer to go and do likewise.

What do you learn from Jesus's words about who is our neighbor?

_____

_____

Key to Jesus's parable is the fact that this was not a Jew helping a Samaritan, but a Samaritan helping a Jew. A Jew who had been ignored by his fellow Jews. The Samaritan not only loved the one who hated him, he risked his own life, showed compassion, bandaged him, carried him to safety, invested his own money to care for him, and received nothing in return.

This is who Jesus chose to display love in action, to capture what it means to truly show mercy. It's not enough to know the law. We must follow the law. It's not enough to say we love our neighbor. We must do it.

Jesus turned the tables on the lawyer, explaining that being a neighbor has nothing to do with geography, citizenship, or race. It has to do with need.[31]

Reread 1 John 3:17–18 and share how John's words confirm Jesus's message in our parable today.

_____

_____

John's words in verses 17 and 18 make the lesson learned in the parable practical and simple.

Love is doing.

Apply It

Read James 2:14–17. John spoke of love and works. What does James speak of in this passage?

_____

_____

How do James's words relate to what we are learning about love?

_____

_____

Read Romans 3:28. Do James's words in the above passage contradict Paul's words in this verse? Explain your answer.

_____

_____

How do faith and love work together?

_____

_____

Good works can never earn salvation because salvation is a free gift from God. But good works are *evidence* of salvation. A deep and abiding faith in Jesus transforms our hearts and minds. A transformed heart enables us to love deeper and greater. It moves us to do good works and makes it easier to put God's love into action.

The takeaway from Jesus's parable is simple: *we are to set aside prejudices and always show love and compassion for our neighbor. And our neighbor is anyone we encounter who has a need.*

The question for us is how do we respond to Jesus's command to love our neighbor.

When is the last time you remember putting love into action? Describe that experience.

_____

_____

_____

Are you as generous as you should be with your time? Gifts and talents? Finances? In what area could you work to be more generous?

_____

_____

_____

Find one way to put love into action in someone else's life this week. Ask God for the specific person who may need this love as well as to show you how to love them. Journal how God worked through your act of love.

_____

_____

Living Love in the Confident Assurance of God's Love

> **MEMORY VERSE:** *Consider the kind of extravagant love the Father has lavished on us—He calls us children of God! It's true; we are His* beloved *children.* (1 John 3:1 The Voice)

What would happen if we lived in the absolute assurance of God's love?

We all *know* God loves us. What I'm talking about is living as if we really, really *believe* it. Believe it deep down to the marrow of our bones. The kind of knowing and believing that leads to a confident assurance that we are daughters of the King! A confidence that stays even when the little voice in our head or the circumstances of our lives scream otherwise. An absolute assurance that allows us to process everything that enters our lives through that filter of God's deep and abiding love.

An assurance that not only allows us to live loved, but also to confidently live out that love.

John speaks to this kind of confidence and assurance as he closes 1 John 3.

Digging Deeper

Read 1 John 3:19–24.

First John 3:19 begins, "*This* is how we know that we belong to the truth" (emphasis added). To what does *this* refer?

_____

_____

Verse 19 continues, "and how we set our hearts at rest in his presence." How do we set our hearts at rest in His presence?

_____

_____

Here's how this verse reads in the New Living Translation: "Our actions will show that we belong to the truth, so we will be confident when we stand before God."

John tells us that our relationship with other people directly affects our relationship with God.

Read Matthew 5:23–24. What does this passage say about relationships?

_____

_____

Broken relationships hinder our communion with the Lord. John provides a formula to protect against broken relationships. It begins with putting love into action.

Before blogs, Facebook, and Pinterest, people had to use hard-copy cookbooks. Old-fashioned cookbooks. When my daughter, Lauren, was young, we created one together . . . a compilation of all the family recipes passed down through the years. One evening, I turned to one of those tattered pages with folded-down corners and found an old favorite.

I labored throughout the day, creating my grandmother's delightful and delicious recipe. I could hardly wait for my family to gather around the table that night. My husband, Monty, usually arrived home on or before 6:30, so that was the appointed time to gather. The kids and I sat down for dinner at 6:30 . . . but no Monty.

6:40 still no Monty.

6:50 . . . still no husband and no call. *Where could he be? So rude.*

By 6:55, when the phone finally did ring, I was fuming! I ignored it. I told my kids to eat. When he finally walked in at 7:00, I greeted him with narrowed eyes and the silent treatment. Not just for that moment, but for the rest of the evening. I was furious. *How could he be so thoughtless? How hard is it to call?*

That night, I chose to nurse my hurt feelings. My anger ruled and reigned over my heart. I was mean, just plain mean. And it felt good.

Ever been there?

I look back now and think how differently this night would have ended had I been equipped to combat my anger and hurt feelings. But I had nothing except my emotions from which to pull, and they ran wild.

What if I had a formula? A process in place to protect me from being led by my emotions?

A formula is a rule or method for doing something. For example, a mathematical formula is group of symbols that express a relationship or are used to solve a problem. Don't even ask me about mathematical symbols! It was my worst subject in school.

But I do know God's Word. Thankfully, it doesn't contain mathematical symbols, but it does contain truths. Truths and promises that when taken together can be used to solve a problem.

Had I had a formula hidden in my heart to speak to the anger that invaded my heart that evening, I would have solved my problem with my husband in a more God-honoring way. His Word would have reined in my out-of-control emotions, silenced my tongue, and even softened my cutting eyes.

Let me replay the night. But this time with a prepared mind, a formula to follow.

6:30 arrives, no Monty. Thoughts seep in: *Where is he? Why hasn't he called? He knows we eat at 6:30 every night. He always calls when he is late.* Anger kicks in as time ticks away.

But then I remember the verses posted above my kitchen sink. I walk over and read them:

Remember, Wendy, a gentle answer turns away wrath, but a harsh word stirs up anger. (Proverbs 15:1)

Wendy, only a fool gives vent to her anger. A wise woman keeps herself under control. You, my daughter, are a wise woman. (Proverbs 29:11)

Wendy, be kind and compassionate to your family. Forgive them, just as I have forgiven you. (Ephesians 4:32)

In the heat of my anger, I look to my formula. To the powerful, life-giving, life-transforming, mind-renewing words of my Savior who only wants the very best for me, my marriage, and my family. When I read them, God reminds me of His character and who He wants me to be. The Holy Spirit softens my heart.

So, when the phone rings at 6:50, I answer it. I hear my husband's sincere apology and accept it. He walks in the door at 7:00, after a long day's work, forgiven and ready to enjoy a wonderful meal with his family . . . experiencing grace, love, forgiveness, and joy.

Which, my friend, is the better scenario?

My formula helped me put love into action. To walk in obedience. Walking in obedience deepens our walk with God. As our walk with God deepens, our confidence in Him strengthens.

Remember we have an enemy in this scenario. He is the deceiver, and he operates in the darkness. He schemes. He prowls. He waits for moments like this to attack, to distract, to divide. But God never leaves us without hope.

In 1 John 3:20, John gives us great hope. Sometimes our heart accuses us. We hear: *You are not strong enough; you deserve better; God doesn't listen to people like you; you'll never change.* Oh, I have heard the accuser whisper that last lie into my heart again and again. I'm so thankful that I no longer believe that lie.

Jeremiah 17:9 describes our hearts in words that are hard to hear: "The human heart is the most deceitful of all things, desperately wicked. Who really knows how bad it is?" (NLT). The answer to that question is God. God knows how wicked our hearts are. And yet, He still loves us, and He is for us.

The enemy of our souls wants us to fight, to fail, to flee. He works hard to draw us away from God. To rob us of the *assurance* of God's unconditional love for us.

John speaks directly to Satan's strategy in verse 20: "Even if we feel guilty, God is greater than our feelings, and he knows everything" (NLT). Our God is love, and He responds in every circumstance and in every way in love. He cannot do anything but love.

Be ever so careful to not allow the devil, *diablos*, the divider, to accuse you and rob you of your confidence. We are daughters of the King. Nothing we do or say will ever take that away. Whenever we make mistakes, lose it, or struggle to forgive, God will forgive us if we confess that sin. We need not, and must not, allow Satan to use confessed sin to accuse us again.

Goodness, sisters, we should never be harder on ourselves than God is. Self-condemnation is not from the Lord.

God knows our hearts. When we confess our sin, He is faithful and just to forgive us our sin . . . to remove it as far as the east is from the west . . . to wash us white as snow (1 John 1:9; Psalm 103:12; Isaiah 1:18)! So, if you are feeling "less than," unworthy, not good enough, remind yourself of who you are (forgiven and redeemed) and Whose you are (a daughter of the King). And greater is He who lives in you than he who lives in the world.

Let's read a story from Peter's life that speaks to this very truth. Peter denied his Lord three times just before Jesus's death. Without a doubt, Peter felt great remorse for his betrayal because Scripture tells us he went outside and wept bitterly. But we see from Jesus's words after His resurrection that He knew Peter's heart. He knew Peter had repented.

Read Luke 22:54–62 and Mark 16:1–8.

Did you notice?

Whose name did he specifically call out?

_____

The angel specially mentioned one name. Of all the disciples, he singled out one. I'm certain hearing those words assured Peter that Jesus not only loved him but also had forgiven him. Although Peter's heart may have condemned him, his Savior had not.

May we receive the same assurance as we surrender our hearts and confess our sin to Jesus.

Are you hearing words of condemnation? Is the evil one speaking lies over your heart and mind? If so, write what you are hearing below. Then write these four letters over what you are hearing: L.I.E.S. Sit for a few minutes with Jesus; pray and confess what is on your heart.

_____

_____

_____

Now write these words: "God is love. God loves me. I am forgiven." Over these words write: T.R.U.T.H.

_____

_____

Read 1 John 3:21–24.

In this passage, John writes that a clear conscience allows us to come before God's throne of grace with confidence. God hears our requests because our hearts are aligned with His. Unburdened hearts allow us to boldly come before our Father. Our confidence lies in knowing we are living in obedience to His commands.

Read 1 Peter 3:7. How does this verse speak to what John teaches here?

_____

_____

Read Psalm 66:18. Same question.

_____

_____

What encouragement, my friend! When we love, when our hearts do not condemn us, we walk rightly with our God. A relationship that assures He hears and answers our prayers.

John writes in 1 John 3:22 that we "receive from him anything we ask." We must read this verse in accordance with a verse we will examine in a later chapter, 1 John 5:14, which says,

> "We live in the bold confidence that God hears our voices when we ask for things that fit His plan." (The Voice)

> "This is the confidence we have in approaching God: that if we ask anything according to his will, he hears us." (NIV)

149

James 4:3 adds another condition for answered prayer. What is it?

_____

_____

_____

Read Psalm 37:4–5, which also adds to our discussion.

What does it mean to "delight yourself in the LORD," and what happens when you do?

_____

_____

What does it mean to "commit your way to the LORD," and what happens when you do?

_____

_____

Summarize what you have learned about prayer in these verses: 1 John 3:21–22; 1 John 5:14; Psalm 37:4–5; James 4:3.

_____

_____

_____

How has what we have studied spoken to you about your prayer life? Are there parts of your prayer life you want to change? If so, what steps will you take to do so?

_____

_____

_____

_____

Apply It

John closes this chapter by again reminding us of Jesus's words on abiding. Jesus spoke thoroughly on this topic so that we would comprehend the value He placed on investing not only our hearts but also our time in our relationship with Him (John 15).

Abiding is key to walking in the confident assurance of God's love and His Word. We comprehend the depth of His love through the sacrifice He made. Abiding helps soften our hearts to His words, even the hard words. Abiding tenders our heart to respond in obedience to the Spirit's conviction. We desire to please Him. We want to obey Him.

Abiding continually exposes our hearts to the character, purposes, and voice of God. It's the daily, systematic feeding of truth that helps align our decisions, our emotions, and our actions with His standard of truth. We filter every decision through the lens of His Word. It helps to ensure we walk in light rather than darkness, to live motivated by love not hate.

Abiding gives us the weapons we need to detect, defeat, and disarm the enemy. To recognize darkness, expose it to light, and claim victory over it!

As we close our week, we have learned God calls us to love others. Of that, there is no doubt. But to live a life of love, we must live loved. What do I mean by this?

To live a life of love, we must first know and believe God loves us fully, perfectly, completely. We cannot love others until we know *and believe* this truth. Jesus manifested His love for us through the greatest sacrifice of all. He gave His life for ours.

True love manifests itself in sacrificial action. It's laying down our lives for another. For whom will we lay down our lives?

We may think we don't have much to give. But, friend, we do. We can speak words of encouragement. We can pray. We can forgive. We can serve. We just need to break out of our routine. Invite God to open our eyes to see how we can live love today.

Small Acts of Love

♥ A smile

♥ An encouraging word

♥ A physical touch

♥ Treating a friend to lunch

♥ Remembering the names of the servers at the businesses you frequent

♥ Sending a prayer or Scripture to a friend

♥ Bringing a meal to a working mom

Where is God calling you to sacrificial giving?

Imagine our world if we all made these expressions of love the pattern of our lives.

What if we let this prayer guide our genesis thoughts . . . our first thoughts . . . of the day?

"Father, help me be a blessing today."

Will you join me in praying this prayer?

If we commit to living and giving love, God will go before us and make a way for us to live love and give love and be a blessing.

Group Discussion Questions

1. Read our verse for today (1 John 3:16) and John 3:16.

   a. Share how they relate to each other.

   b. What does it look like in today's world to lay down our lives for our brothers and sisters?

   c. Why do we find it hard to sacrifice our needs and desires for another?

2. Do you remember a specific time when you laid down your life for another?

   a. What did God ask you to sacrifice (time, pride, finances, relationship)?

   b. What was the result for you and the one for whom you made that sacrifice?

3. Read Ephesians 1:3–14.

   a. Because love found its way to the cross, we are the beneficiaries of some pretty amazing blessings. List at least six spiritual blessings you find in this passage.

   b. Which blessing has impacted your life most?

4. Read Galatians 5:22–26.

   a. List the fruit of the Spirit.

   b. God gave us His fruit (and our spiritual blessings) so that we can live loved . . . live out His love right where He has us. What prevents you from living in the fullness of His blessings and fruit?

5. Jesus teaches that true love manifests itself in sacrificial action. We closed today's lesson talking about living in the pattern of love. Part of that includes beginning our day with a prayer inviting God into that pattern. In addition to praying the morning prayer, what is one step you can take today to begin living in the pattern of love?

WEEK

FOUR

WALK IN FAITH

PRAYER: *Heavenly Father, I confess that my perception of love is so vastly different from Yours. Oftentimes I view people's actions through the lens of my wounded soul. I sift people's words through the hurt piled up in my heart. I know deep down inside that I don't understand Your love. Help me surrender my inaccurate, preconceived notions of love. Open my heart to receive and embrace authentic love . . . Your love . . . the kind of love that laid down its life for me. Enable me to comprehend the vastness of this love. Soak it deep into the marrow of my bones so that it becomes one with my soul, and I truly live loved. And then transform my heart from the inside out with Your love so that I can be a glowing example of Your lovingkindness. Through the power of Your Holy Spirit, enable me to walk in that love, in any situation, in any relationship, anytime, anywhere. Help me to believe the best and forgive the worst. May I reflect the fruit of Your love in all I say and do. I ask this in Jesus's precious name. Amen.*

To Believe or Not to Believe

MEMORY VERSE: *You, dear children, are from God and have overcome them, because the one who is in you is greater than the one who is in the world.* (1 John 4:4)

Okay, are you seeing a theme here? Love . . . love . . . and more love.

This doesn't mean that John has run out of ideas on what to write. Each teaching presents love from a different perspective. First, John defines what it means to live in fellowship with our Father and how that relates to living in light versus living in darkness (1 John 2). Second, John reassures us that we are beloved children of God . . . that we live loved so that we can live out that love to the world around us (1 John 3).

And now, John takes us to even more challenging teachings: warning against false teachers and spirits who seek to hinder and hijack that love.

1 John

Digging Deeper

Read 1 John 4:1–6.

Before we dive in, let's frame this teaching with a bit of background. At the time of John's writing, the New Testament had not yet been completed, and that which had been written had not been widely circulated. Consequently, each individual church depended heavily on local leaders and teachers to teach them truth. John was concerned with the false teachers that had been infiltrating the churches. Paul addressed this same issue in 1 Thessalonians 5:19–21.

Read 1 Thessalonians 5:19–21. What was Paul's concern?

_____

_____

As discussed earlier, John repeatedly sought to expose and guard against false teachers. His concern still applies for our churches today. Stories periodically appear in the media claiming Jesus was married, had children, or did not rise from the dead.

John sets forth a test to help his spiritual children discern truth from lies. Read 1 John 4:1:

"My dear friends, don't believe everything you hear. Carefully weigh and examine what people tell you. Not everyone who talks about God comes from God. There are a lot of lying preachers loose in the world." (The Message)

John writes his command using the present tense. It literally means to stop an act already in progress: "stop believing." His choice of wording indicates the churches had already been taken in by these false teachings.

But before we judge too quickly, we too can be guilty of the same.

Our culture tends to present the "feel good" part of religion and often leaves out the hard stuff of faith. John advocates healthy skepticism when it comes to spiritual claims. He carefully chose his words, using the terms *weigh* and *examine* to invite us to prove and scrutinize what we hear and see.

In Greek, we find two terms for such testing. The first, *peirazo*, carries with it the connotation of examining someone for the purpose of finding fault. The second, *dokimazo*, is a metallurgist term for testing the **authenticity** of a substance. The metal tester exposes metal to fire, and as the fire heats up, it burns off everything except that which is pure metal.[32]

Similarly, we should be continually testing the spirits to see whether they are truly from God. Our goal should *not* be faultfinding and judging. Rather, we should conduct a humble, sincere assessment of the messages, thinking the best of our teacher unless proven otherwise.

What are we to test (1 John 4:1)?

_____

_____

How do we know if a teacher's spirit is from God (verse 2)? Explain what John says in your own words.

_____

_____

What are some other ways to "test the spirits"?

_____

_____

Clearly, we should not believe everything we hear. The fact that a man or woman stands in a pulpit does not guarantee he has been called by God. It doesn't guarantee she speaks a Spirit-inspired message grounded in biblical truth. We must give careful attention to his or her words and align them with God's infallible, written Word.

How do we test their words?

A good litmus test is determining whether they teach that Jesus is fully God and fully man. The Gnostics did not believe this. And today, some still deny Jesus's incarnation and resurrection. Others accept His humanity but not His divinity, saying He was a great teacher but not divine.

We must align our teacher's words with Jesus's words. Jesus made some bold claims: He was God and man; fully human and fully divine; left heaven and came to earth; was born of a virgin; grew into a man; died a real death; rose from the dead; returned to earth in His resurrected body; ascended into heaven; sent the Holy Spirit power to indwell His people; will return one day as Judge; has always been and always will be.

Satan doesn't want us to know and believe these truths because they equip and empower us to defeat his lies and deception and ensure abundant, victorious living.

Satan has many tactics. He is a clever one. He rarely engages in an all-out assault against us. His tactics are subtler. His antichrists infiltrate our churches and communities using deception to lure us away from truth. The false teachers comingle truth with their lies. Satan knows this is a far more effective way to entice people than direct contradiction.

Read Matthew 7:15–20. How do Jesus's words here speak into John's teaching?

_____

_____

Read 1 John 4:3. What does John say about those who do not confess these truths about Jesus?

_____

_____

In summary, the first test to determine the validity of a teacher of the Word is to examine his or her theology. What does this person teach about Jesus? If their teaching aligns with the truths of Christ's teaching about His identity, the teacher passes the litmus test.

It has become increasingly politically correct to affirm that all monotheistic religions (religions that believe in one god) worship the same God.

But that statement is a lie. Why? Because none of those other religions believe that Jesus is God's Son. They do not believe in the triune God (Father, Son, and Holy Spirit). And they do not believe Jesus is the only way to God. Yet, Jesus made it quite clear: "I am the way and the truth and the life. No one comes to the Father except through me" (John 14:6).

Some criticize Jesus's words as presenting a road that is too narrow by claiming that He is the *only* way. I beg to differ. Jesus's way is wide . . . open to the whole world. Anyone . . . no matter race, nationality, gender, or age . . . no matter their past or present . . . can come to Jesus. He holds His arms wide open to welcome all who say yes to His amazing gift of salvation.

So, if a teacher does *not* agree with any of the doctrinal truths above, John writes that he is *not* of God. That teacher is influenced by the spirit of antichrist. It is false teaching that denies and is contrary to biblical truth.

The distinction is clear. The line is drawn.

Apply It

John isn't the only writer to warn against antichrists. Scripture is very clear that antichrists, fed by antichristian spirits opposed to God's Holy Spirit and His truth, will rise and fall throughout history. In the last days, one eminent Antichrist will engage in an all-out war against Christ. The lesser antichrists, of which John speaks, prepare the way for the great and final Antichrist.

For more on the antichrists, read 2 Thessalonians 2:3–12 and Revelation 13.

Paul wrote these words to the Thessalonian believers to encourage them about Jesus's second coming. Paul knew the pressures they faced. The persecution. The false teachers. The temptation to walk away from their faith. Paul wanted to equip the young church with truth so that they could stand firm amid these trials.

Antichrists have existed in every generation, and will continue to rise in generations yet to come, to wreak havoc on this earth. Just before Christ's second coming, the last and final Antichrist, "the man of lawlessness," will arise as Satan's final tool, fully empowered and mobilized by his evil.

Paul warns of him and Scripture teaches about him so that we will be ready. If our faith is strong, if we are grounded in sound doctrine, we need not be afraid of what lies ahead because we are sons and daughters of the One True God. The man of lawlessness is a defeated foe because of Jesus's work on the cross at Calvary. No matter how powerful he becomes or how horrific his tactics or how hopeless our world may seem, we need not fear because God is always and forever in control.

Bible study equips us to distinguish truth from lies. When we read or hear something that doesn't feel right, our assignment is to line it up with biblical truth and invite the Holy Spirit to confirm it. If the teaching doesn't align with God's truth, the abiding presence of the Holy Spirit will cause an uneasiness to invade our hearts. We will know.

Read and study any of the following passages: John 1:1–4, 14, 17; John 3:16; John 10:30, 38; John 11:25; John 14:1–3, 23; Galatians 4:4–5; 1 John 1:1–3. Which of these truths about Jesus particularly stand out to you right now?

_____

_____

_____

The Example of God's Love

MEMORY VERSE: *You, dear children, are from God and have overcome them, because the one who is in you is greater than the one who is in the world.* (1 John 4:4)

Several years ago, my dear friend Bobbie received the news that she had stage four ovarian cancer. My heart ached. My mind reeled. Disillusioned by the news, questions set in.

Why her?

Why now?

She is one of Your shining stars on this earth; how could You allow this to happen?

God had crossed our paths eight years before when I was teaching a young women's Bible study in Charlotte. The leadership had scheduled a year-end celebration. I awakened that morning feeling ill and didn't want to go. However, I had committed to share at the event, which obligated me to attend. I went with a heavy heart and grumpy spirit.

Afterward, a mutual friend introduced me to Bobbie. She lived in Florida but "happened" to be in town visiting that week. Jesus radiated from her bright eyes and infectious smile. Kind and encouraging words flowed from her lips through every conversation. Our hearts connected immediately. She invited me to lunch, and we spent the afternoon sharing mom-and-ministry stories.

It also "so happened" that her husband, Robert, was a literary agent. He walked through the door moments before I headed out to pick up my son. We spoke briefly, and I left. Little did I know what God had planned just around the corner.

Bobbie contacted me the following week and asked for sample chapters of a book I had written. A book that I had already submitted for publication and had been rejected numerous times. After reading the chapters, she convinced her husband to review them. He agreed, and even though he wasn't taking new clients, he called and offered to represent me in my search to find a publisher for my book. This was a door that only God (and Bobbie) could have opened.

If you have read my first book, *Hidden Joy,* or been touched by its teachings, Bobbie's love, tenacity, and generosity made it possible.

After doctors diagnosed Bobbie with stage four ovarian cancer, prayer and heavy doses of chemotherapy and radiation kept the cancer at bay for two years. But then it returned with a vengeance.

After hearing the news, I flew to Florida to spend some precious time with my friend to encourage and love on her. Not surprisingly, it was Bobbie who encouraged and loved on me. We shared a delightful lunch of chicken salad, fresh fruit, and her favorite pasta dish. Over lunch, she imparted more of her invaluable wisdom. Bobbie's generosity to pour into me during her toughest battle blessed me beyond words. She praised God through word and song and spoke God's Word over and into my life. She reminded me again of what I needed to honor and treasure in my life above all else.

I want to share her words with you today. I pray they bless and encourage you as they did me:

Wendy, nothing else equals the hope you find in loving and knowing Jesus with all your heart.

Wendy, the truth, strength, and treasures you find in God's Word are supreme above all else the world offers.

Wendy, the call to love your husband and your children is your highest calling, above your career, writing, ministry, and friends.

Wendy, take time to praise and worship God throughout your day . . . listening to and singing hymns and spiritual songs.

I never appreciated old hymns until I met Bobbie. How I wish you could have heard her sing. She sang them with such passion. Because of her love for hymns, I learned to love and appreciate them like never before.

Bobbie modeled courage and grace. She shined the love of Jesus to all she met because she *knew* the depths of His love down to the marrow of her bones. Even in her most trying days, during chemo treatments, plagued by nausea, mouth sores, and indescribable pain, Bobbie live loved and shared the love of Christ. She opened her Bible and shared the gospel with nurses, attendants, fellow patients and their families, doctors, and surgeons.

So, when I received the news of Bobbie's passing, again questions rushed in . . . *Why her? Why now? She loved lavishly. She praised ferociously. She sang angelically. She gave generously. Why didn't You heal her?*

It is the closing words in her last letter to me that settled my heart.

"With the ending of my cancer treatments and the hope of heaven, Jesus has been very near and very real. Scripture verses have come to my memory, bringing a deep sense of peace . . . and gratitude for Jesus's gift of forgiveness, restoration, and eternal life with Him. When our family was visiting recently, I was reminded of an old hymn that paints the picture of how this redemption has been sealed. Our Abby [her granddaughter] sat down and sang it with me.

'And when before the throne, I stand in Him complete.
Jesus died my soul to save, my lips shall still repeat.
Jesus paid it all, all to Him I owe.
Sin had left a crimson stain; He washed it white as snow.'"

Bobbie's life will have a ripple effect on generations. Her children and their children. My children and their children. Oh, how I want to live and love like Bobbie. She read through the Bible many times. She memorized Scripture. She prayed fervently. She worshiped regularly. She gave generously. Not because she wanted to impress anyone, but because she knew she was loved deeply by her Savior, and she loved Him deeply back. She shared that love wherever her feet carried her. Jesus's love flowed so evidently and magnificently it left a sweet aroma wherever she wandered.

Lord, I thank You for Bobbie's life and the love she shared . . . for her loving husband, Robert . . . for her lovely girls who mirror their mama's example in so many ways . . . and for all the lives she has touched that will now go forth and spill Your grace and love in ways that will change the world.

This is why I have dedicated this book to Bobbie!

Digging Deeper

Bobbie's story beautifully sets us up for our next passage from 1 John.
Read 1 John 4:7–8. What word opens verse 7?

_____

_____

John opens this passage of Scripture addressing his children, "[d]ear friends." *Agapetoi* in Greek means "divinely loved ones."[33] Paraphrasing John's words, "Loved ones, you who are divinely loved ought to love one another." We who are loved by God should love each other. God first loved us so that we can know real love and then love others with that same divine love.

From where does this love come?

_____

_____

Describe God's love.

_____

_____

Why is it so hard for us to love with God's love?

_____

_____

Love distinguishes Christianity from every other world religion because no other religion has sacrificial love as the driving force behind its beliefs. You see, love originates with our God. It's an integral part of His being. He is its source, its only source.

Noted Christian apologist, philosopher, and author Frances Schaeffer shared the following in the introduction of his book, *The Mark of a Christian:*

> *Through the centuries men have displayed many different symbols to show that they are Christians. They have worn marks in the lapels of their coats, hung chains around their necks, even had special haircuts.*
>
> *Of course, there is nothing wrong with any of this, if one feels it is his calling. But there is a much better sign—a mark that has not been thought up just as a matter of expediency for use on some special occasion or in some specific era. It is a universal mark that is to last through all the ages of the church till Jesus comes back.*
>
> *What is this mark?*

At the close of his ministry, Jesus looks forward to his death on the cross, the open tomb and the ascension. Knowing that he is about to leave, Jesus prepares his disciples for what is to come. It is here that he makes clear what will be the distinguishing mark of the Christian:

Little children, yet a little while I am with you. Ye shall seek me: and as I said unto the Jews, Whither I go, ye cannot come; so now I say to you. A new commandment I give unto you, that ye love one another; as I have loved you, that ye also love one another. By this all men know that ye are my disciples, if ye have love one to another. (John 13:33–35 KJV) [34]

God's love marks us, friend, always and forever. Jesus poured out His blood on the cross to show us how much He loves us. What He asks in return is that our hearts now pour forth that same love to others.

Sometimes loving is just plain hard. But God doesn't ask or expect us to love in our own strength. He knows that is impossible. We need His help. We receive that help when God implants His Spirit in us. It is through the indwelling presence of His Spirit that we receive His very nature. It's that nature in us that enables us to love with His incredible love. His nature comes alive in us and empowers us to do what alone our flesh could not do.

Doesn't that just blow your mind? God literally imparts His love so that we can love others with His perfect love.

Read Romans 5:5; Galatians 5:22–23; and 1 Peter 1:22. How do these passages speak to the truths we are learning today?

_____

_____

Friend, Jesus is the perfect model of the love that God commands. If we observe how Jesus loved, if we notice who He loved, we will know better how to love. Though we will never love to the degree Jesus loved—because He is the living manifestation of God's love—through the indwelling power of His Spirit, we can sacrificially love despite the pull of our flesh and emotions.

Apply It

Love is a valid test of our faith. If we know that we are sons and daughters of the King, we know His divine nature lives and thrives in us. And that divine nature includes love. Our God equips us to love one another with His love. If we find ourselves struggling with that love, we need to ask ourselves if we truly understand the depths of His love for us.

May the truths below remind you of the depths of God's love for you:

♥ You are forgiven (Romans 8:1; 5:11).

♥ You are a beloved child of God (Galatians 3:26).

♥ You are a new creation (2 Corinthians 5:17).

♥ You are God's treasured possession (Exodus 19:5; Deuteronomy 26:18).

♥ Your name is engraved on the palm of His hand (Isaiah 49:16).

♥ You are known by God (Psalm 139:13–16; Matthew 10:31).

Know these truths.
Believe these truths.
Walk in these truths.

Friend, if you struggle with one (or more) of these promises, invite God to bring it alive in your heart. Each truth affirms your identity in Christ and draws you closer and closer to the Father's heart and to internalizing His unfathomable love for you.

Each one ensures you can trust God more and more with the hard stuff of life . . . like Bobbie did.

Each one deepens your walk with Him, transforming your heart to be more and more like His.

Each one enables you to love in the way He created and calls us to love. The best way to summarize what we have learned is this:

God *is* love. We *do* love!

Let me repeat that.

God is love. We do love.

Write a prayer asking God to help you "do love" with a person who is a challenge for you to love. Ask Him to fill you full of unconditional, sacrificial love for that individual and an avenue to practically live that out. Now here's the hard part. Take one step toward expressing your love today.

_____

_____

_____

_____

_____

The Expression of God's Love

MEMORY VERSE: *You, dear children, are from God and have overcome them, because the one who is in you is greater than the one who is in the world.* (1 John 4:4)

Are you working on this week's memory verse? Tuck this promise deep in your heart for when life's circumstances overwhelm you. Greater is the One who lives and moves in you than the one who prowls around you, the one who seeks to destroy the perfect plan that the greater One has for you.

Digging Deeper

Read 1 John 4:9–11.

Again, John continues his message on love. This time he focuses on our response to God's love.

1 John

Share *your* thoughts on God's love.

_____

_____

God's love is not abstract or theoretical; it's concrete and tangible. It announced its arrival two thousand years ago when God unmistakably demonstrated His love for us by sending "His only Son" into our world.

God initiated this love. We did nothing. It poured forth from the heart of the One who *is* Love.

Most religions require their followers to "do" something to receive their god's love and attention. Typically, they must pursue their god or gods and then follow many rules and regulations to stay in good standing with that god or gods.

Our God turns that formula upside down. In Christianity, God does the seeking, not His people. And He seeks them, not when they are good and obedient—following all the rules—but when they are steeped in the deepest, darkest places of sin and rebellion. Our God loves fallen, broken, hurting, wounded, imperfect people. He comes into their lives and rescues them so that He can usher them into a new life and a new relationship. It's an absolutely, beautiful, unconditional love that is unmatched.

How is the love of God manifested in us (1 John 4:9)?

_____

_____

Read Isaiah 53:4–6. What did Isaiah prophesy in this passage?

_____

_____

The big word we find in some translations of 1 John 4:9 is *propitiation*. God sent His Son to be the propitiation for our sin. This word derives from the Greek *hilasmos* and means "satisfied" or "satisfaction." Jesus's shed blood satisfied the debt that needed to be paid for our sin.

Because God is love and God is holy, His love and holiness require that He act justly and judge sin. God's wrath is His love in action judging sin.

We find another formula here.

God's wrath demands justice.

God's justice demands punishment.

There are only two ways to satisfy God's wrath.

God's wrath is satisfied either when *unrepentant, unbelieving* sinners *reject* Jesus's sacrificial death on the cross or when *repentant, believing* sinners *accept* Jesus's sacrificial death on the cross. The first sinner receives eternal punishment; the latter, eternal salvation.

The good news is that what Christ accomplished on the cross is available for *all* people. Not just a chosen few. Christ's work on the cross redeems *all* who repent and believe. We are all sinners and deserve God's wrath (Romans 3:10). But God loved His children so much He sent Christ to take our place. To take our wrath upon Him. To take the punishment we deserved. He substituted Jesus for you and for me.

Jesus's sacrifice was sufficient to cover all sin for all people for all time. There is redeeming power in His blood. It's a mystery we will never understand, but Christ's blood purifies us from all sin and washes us clean (1 John 1:7).

Read Romans 5:8–11. **What does Jesus's blood do for us now and in the future?**

What does it mean to you to be "reconciled" and have "peace" with God?

God's gift of unconditional love demands a response from us.

1 John

What is that response (1 John 4:11)?

_____

_____

We have touched on this topic before. There are people in this world that we find just plain hard to love. It might be a family member, a friend, a coworker, a boss, a committee member, a neighbor, but most especially an enemy. We know God asks that we love "everyone," but honestly, we cannot imagine loving *that* person . . . ever . . . under any circumstances.

Think of someone you find hard to love. What is it about that person that makes him or her hard to love?

_____

_____

The truth is that we cannot fully love people out of our own love tank. In part, because we lack the necessary resources in our fallen nature to love that deeply and that unconditionally. But also in part, because our culture revolves on the principle of reciprocity. Be good to those who are good to you. If a neighbor helps us out in a bind, we reply in kind. If someone invites us for dinner, we return the invitation. If a parent drives carpool for us because we had surgery, we offer to do the same. If our boss honors us at a staff meeting for a job well done, we work more diligently to show appreciation for the recognition. It's good manners. It's expected. And most of all, it makes loving others easy. It comes naturally. We don't mind being kind to those who are kind to us.

But, what about when . . .

♥ Your neighbor yells at your children every time they step even one foot into the neighbor's yard, even when no damage is done?

♥ You drive your friend's kid to practice and back . . . every day . . . every week . . . all season and never hear the words *thank you*?

♥ You work your tail off on a project, and at the company-wide meeting your boss presents the project as his own, and the president of the company loves it and gives your boss all the credit?

♥ Your coworker always drinks your diet cola in the fridge at work and never replenishes your supply or even acknowledges that she drinks it?

Loving is no longer so easy, is it?

And yet, we are called to love . . . even when the actions and words of another prove thoughtless, unappreciative, and unkind.

We cannot possibly do this on our own.

If our view of love is "what will I get," it will fail us every time. If our view of love is "what will I give," it will never fail.

Love is a choice. We must choose to give it . . . period.

Godly love only works when we allow God to work His love in and through us.

What does this love look like?

Unconditional

First, God's love is unconditional. We are to love people *despite* all the reasons we can list *not* to love them. Remember Romans 5:8? God demonstrated His love for us in that while we were sinners (while we were rotten, rebellious, prideful, selfish people), Christ died for us. He loved us when there was nothing lovable about us. Oh friend, we are never more like God than when we love an unlovable person. We will never feel God's pleasure more than when we love someone who's unkind, thoughtless, or unappreciative.

When we don't extend this kind of love, we look exactly like the world. We are no different.

God calls us to be different . . . to be set apart. To be a shining light in this generation. "In the same way, let your light shine before others, that they may see your good deeds and glorify your Father in heaven" (Matthew 5:16).

Sacrificial

Second, God's love is sacrificial. It is a giving love. A selfless love. An active love. We can speak words of love to someone, but it isn't until we *show* God's love that they truly experience and know His love.

Jesus made the ultimate sacrificial gift when He gave up His glory, His honor, His life to free us from our sin and certain death.

It's a love that doesn't keep score.

What does that love look like for you and me? It might be baking Christmas cookies and taking them to your unfriendly neighbor. It might mean writing your prideful boss a note sharing how you appreciate working for the company and how thankful you are that they are investing in you. It may entail driving carpool the remainder of the season, expecting nothing in return, trusting your friend's schedule is overwhelmed and she needs your help.

Apply It

Friend, we are the earthly vessels God uses to reveal His heavenly love.

Our neighbors may never walk through the doors of a church, but they will walk through the doors of our homes.

Our friends may never open the Bible to learn what's in God's heart, but they will join in a conversation with us to learn what's in our hearts.

We make God real. We are His ambassadors. Let's represent our Father well!

As we close, think again of the name the Lord brought to mind earlier. The one you find hard to love. The person you can't believe the Lord would ask you to love. I have that name in my mind right now. And I can tell you with confidence that the Lord is calling me to love that person. But He is not asking me to love her in my strength, and He is not asking you to love your hard-to-love person in your strength. He is asking us to love that person in His strength. So, let's take time to meditate on God's unconditional, sacrificial love and invite Him to fill our love tank so we can love our unlovable one in and through His strength.

Abba Father, thank You for loving me, a most unlovable girl at times. Thank You for forgiving me of all my sin and giving me new life in You. Thank You that in You I am a new creation. Fill my reservoir of love to overflowing with Your unconditional, sacrificial love.

Through that love, enable me to love [name]. Help me to let go of my hurt [bitterness, anger, unforgiveness, betrayal, resentment] in a way that only You can accomplish. Bind up and heal my heart so that I can be a vessel of Your love for [name]. Empower me to love [name] with Your love. And as I love [name] with Your love, open her heart so she can know and experience You and Your love in her life. I ask this in Jesus's name. Amen.

Now let's you and I commit to one act, one word, one way to love our unlovable person today!

The Empowerment of God's Love

> **MEMORY VERSE:** *You, dear children, are from God and have overcome them, because the one who is in you is greater than the one who is in the world.* (1 John 4:4)

Let's travel back in time and join Jesus and His disciples in the "Upper Room." At this dinner, the disciples had no idea the pain, suffering, and devastation lurking just around the corner. But Jesus did.

He knew His hour had come.

He knew it was the final time He would gather with His friends.

He knew one among them would betray Him.

Most importantly, as hard as this was, He knew He was walking in His Father's will.

In the shadow of the cross, Jesus poured out His heart like never before. His words and His actions confused the disciples. He washed their feet. He spoke difficult, confusing truths. He predicted one among them would betray Him (John 13). He told them He would be leaving them to join His Father. He said He would prepare a place for them. He encouraged them not to worry because He was *the Way* to that place and to His Father, and they knew that Way (John 14).

Jesus knew the thought of His leaving them frightened them. He knew they would feel alone and abandoned. To calm their hearts, He gave them a great promise. A promise to bring great hope.

Read John 14:16–17. What was Jesus's promise?

_____

_____

Read John 14:17, 26; 15:26; 16:8, 13–14. What did Jesus teach about the Holy Spirit?

_____

_____

What would your thoughts have been if you had been in that room and heard Jesus's words about the gifting of the Holy Spirit?

_____

_____

What are your feelings now about the Holy Spirit? What is His purpose in our lives?

_____

_____

Do you see the Holy Spirit at work in your midst? Do you receive power from His presence in your life? If you answered no to these questions, share why.

_____

_____

I'm sure Jesus's words baffled the disciples. He told them He was leaving, yet He declared He would still live among them.

Let's take a closer look at a few other words Jesus spoke, words spoken *after* His death and resurrection.

Read John 20:22.

Not until I was preparing for this lesson did Jesus's words in John 20 come alive for me. Words I'm guessing came alive for His disciples as they remembered the words He had spoken in John 14.

Don't miss the miracle found in His words: "Now He [Jesus] drew close enough to each of them that *they could feel His breath*. He breathed on them: 'Welcome the Holy Spirit of the Living God'" (John 20:22 The Voice).

Read those words again, sweet friend. Soak them in. "Now He [Jesus] drew close enough to each of them that *they could feel His breath*. He breathed on them: 'Welcome the Holy Spirit of the Living God'" (John 20:22 The Voice).

Jesus exhaled, and with that single breath, the Spirit of the Living God entered each of His beloved friends, rushing through their bodies, filling them full. Can you even imagine what they must have experienced in that moment?

Through the divine breath of heaven's own Son, God not only imparted spiritual, eternal life but also empowered them to do His work on this earth!

Digging Deeper

Read 1 John 4:12–16.

John dedicated several chapters to God's love as demonstrated by both the Father and His Son.

Don't just read these truths. Learn them. Memorize them. Believe them. Live them with all your heart.

♥ Jesus's *life* unveiled the *character* of God.

♥ Jesus's *death* revealed the *love* of God.

♥ Jesus's *resurrection* displayed the *power* of God.

In 1 John 4:12–16, John emphasized another aspect of God's love, the third part of the Trinity. The gifting of His Holy Spirit. John underscored how love finds its source in not just one . . . not just two . . . but in all three parts of the Godhead.

God's Spirit lives in each one of us because the moment we invite Jesus to be our Lord and Savior, He seals us with His Spirit. God's love lives in us through the Holy Spirit because love is a fruit of His Spirit. Love abides in us because God abides in us (Galatians 5:22–23).

Ephesians 1:13–14 explains:

"And you also were included in Christ when you heard the message of truth, the gospel of your salvation. When you believed, you were marked in him with a seal, the promised Holy Spirit, who is a deposit guaranteeing our inheritance until the redemption of those who are God's possession—to the praise of his glory."

What happens the moment we confess our sins and accept Jesus as our Lord and Savior? Describe *your* thoughts as to what spiritually happened in your heart and life in that moment.

_____

_____

If you've accepted Jesus, how has this promised gift become a reality in your life?

_____

_____

What does John mean in 1 John 4:12 when he teaches that "if we love one another, God lives in us and his love is made complete in us"?

_____

_____

When God comes to live inside us, we partake "of His Spirit." The Greek rendering of the words *of His Spirit—ek tou pneumatos—*suggests that we actually participate in the Spirit of God; literally, "He has given us out of His Spirit."

We see this same construction in 1 John 3:24. When we love, we draw that love from God's Spirit. [35]

Our Spirit-led obedience to love another, especially one who is difficult to love, is compelling evidence that we are indwelled and driven by something greater than ourselves. A higher power that overrides our fallen earthly flesh.

Grasp the import of this truth in our corrupt, narcissistic world. When we love one another, we manifest, or make real, a God whose divine nature will never again be seen this side of heaven. We put our God on display. We make an unseen God visible to those who are drowning in hopelessness, crushed by grief, paralyzed by fear, incapacitated by anxiety, lost in sin.

We not only have the answer, but we know the One *with* all the answers.

When we live out God's love,

we model forgiveness for the one struggling to forgive;

we offer hope to the one who is hopeless;

we provide comfort for the one who is grieving;

we hold the key to one imprisoned by fear;

we point the lost to the One who created them.

God's Spirit equips and empowers us to love them all!

1 John

Read 1 John 4:13. John writes "This is how we _____ that we live in him and he in us." Complete the blank and then note what the last part of this verse says.

_____

_____

The word *know* is the Greek *ginōskō*, "to know by experience." When we experience the Holy Spirit's work in our lives, we know His indwelling presence is real. He enables us to do what on our own we just couldn't do.

The Spirit is a living, breathing gift from God, indwelling our bodies. Don't miss this! The Spirit's presence in us ensures we have continuous, nonstop fellowship with God. This is not a temporary filling. The Spirit takes up permanent residence (2 John 1:1–2). He is in us to stay, forever and ever!

Apply It

Let's dig a bit deeper into the work of the Holy Spirit.

Read Ezekiel 37:1–14. Say in your own words what happens in this story as God works through Ezekiel.

_____

_____

_____

How I love this story! So many rich lessons to learn from the Valley of Dry Bones passage. The one for today is how God chooses to partner with His children to do kingdom work. He waits for us to make ourselves available to Him so He can work through us to release His power on this earth! Make sure you get this. The God of the universe wants to partner with you and me to accomplish His heavenly purposes. He did it with Moses, David, Ezekiel, Peter, Paul, and so many more.

God desires to build His kingdom through us and has empowered us to make it happen. We need only make ourselves available and walk in that power!

Below are more verses about the Holy Spirit. Note what you learn about the Spirit's ministry and work in our lives.

♥ **Ezekiel 36:27**

_____

_____

♥ **Acts 1:1–9**

_____

_____

♥ **Philippians 4:13**

_____

_____

♥ **1 Corinthians 12:4–7, 11**

_____

_____

♥ **Galatians 5:22–23**

_____

_____

Let's revisit the opening of today's lesson when the disciples learned from Jesus's own lips about His departure and that hard times lie ahead for them. Dejection set in. The call Jesus placed upon their lives to carry on the baton of faith guaranteed hatred, rejection, and persecution.

Jesus, knowing their fears and emotions, encouraged His disciples with these words:

> *"I know that hearing news like this is overwhelming and sad. But the truth is that My departure will be a gift that will serve you well, because if I don't leave, the great Helper will not come to your aid. When I leave I will send Him to you"* (John 16:6–7 The Voice).

Jesus kept His promise. His very name is Immanuel, which means "God with us"! Sending Jesus had been God's game plan all along. He never intended to leave His people alone. Throughout His Word, God promises that He will never leave us or forsake us! He will be with us to the end of the age.

Read Romans 8:28, 31–39. What hope do the truths in this passage give you for your circumstances or for the circumstances of someone you love? Choose a few of the scriptural promises that have spoken to you, write them out, memorize them, and pray them. Invite the Holy Spirit to come alive in you and in your situation and do a mighty work!

_____

_____

_____

Casting Out Fear

> **MEMORY VERSE:** *You, dear children, are from God and have overcome them, because the one who is in you is greater than the one who is in the world.* (1 John 4:4)

*N*ow we spend time with some of my most favorite verses in 1 John, verses that speak to an emotion that held me captive for over a decade. Fear. And I know that I'm not alone.

The dictionary defines *fear* this way: "a distressing emotion aroused by impending danger, evil, pain, etc., whether the threat is real or imagined; the feeling or condition of being afraid."

Did you catch the words describing *threat*? Real *or imagined*.

A friend once sent me this acronym for fear . . . **F**alse **E**vidence **A**ppearing **R**eal.

Do you notice any similarities in the two?

Many of us live controlled by fear. It often arises in the form of a *condition* . . . something bad *might* happen. It's the "what if." My plane *might* go down in midair. My mammogram *might* reveal cancer. I *might* lose my job. My child *might* get kidnapped. My husband *might* be having an affair. We *might* not be able to pay our bills.

Most of the time, our "conditional might" has no basis in reality. It finds its roots in something from our past, something we have read online or seen on television. It looms large in our imagination and eventually activates a state of heightened anxiety.

Whether we fear the known or the unknown, fear is a thief. Like a runaway train, it steals our joy, our peace, our contentedness. It robs us of sleep. And in its extreme state, fear prevents us from living God's promised abundant life.

I asked some friends to share their fears . . .

♥ *I fear I'm not good enough; I won't fit in.*

♥ *I fear I'll never measure up to the woman (wife, mother . . . fill in the blank) God and everyone else want me to be.*

♥ *I fear I'll never find anyone to love me.*

♥ *I fear I'll let people down.*

♥ *I fear my husband will leave me.*

♥ *I fear I won't get into the college I want.*

♥ *I fear my husband is having an affair.*

♥ *I just graduated from college, and I fear I'll never find a job.*

♥ *I'm afraid of flying.*

♥ *I'm afraid of spiders.*

♥ *I'm afraid none of this (God, Jesus) is real.*

♥ *I fear my children getting hurt or very sick, being kidnapped, failing, making wrong choices.*

♥ *I fear losing my baby.*

♥ *I fear I'm not a good parent; afraid I've messed up and it's too late to repair the damage.*

♥ *I fear letting go of my children and letting them grow into who God made them to be instead of who I want them to be.*

♥ *I fear living for Jesus will alienate my friends and family and leave me feeling alone and isolated.*

♥ *I fear my family will not come to know Jesus as their Lord and Savior.*

♥ *I fear rejection.*

♥ *I fear the future as I face my empty nest.*

♥ *I fear my husband dying.*

♥ *I fear dying prematurely or suffering a catastrophic illness that would leave my family without me or having to care for me.*

♥ *I fear my husband will lose his job.*

♥ *I fear we won't have money at the end of the month to pay our bills.*

Do you find any of your fears in this list? I saw mine.

List *your* fears. How do you feel when you are afraid?

_____

_____

How do you cope with your fear? How has that coping mechanism worked?

_____

_____

Digging Deeper

My friends' responses comforted me, really. I learned that I'm not alone. We all have fears.

Fears are inescapable because we have an enemy. You know his name. He pounces on those places of insecurity and anxiety and magnifies them until they become fears . . . sometimes paralyzing fears.

As children of the One True God, we know that we are overcomers. Romans 8:37 tells us, "No, in all these things we are more than conquerors through him who loved us." Not just conquerors but MORE than conquerors.

Our challenge, and my goal for us as daughters of the King, is to believe this truth so deeply that we not only combat our fears but fully and completely overcome them!

Scripture gives us a process:

Step One: Recognize and confess your fear.

Step Two: Analyze and understand your fear and from where it comes.

Step Three: Identify a biblical truth to combat and overcome that fear.

Consider the list of fears above and your own. Did you notice that nearly all are "conditional mights," meaning they are future-based? They have not happened yet, but they might happen. They are "maybes." It's more likely than not that they won't happen, but we still fear them.

That fear of the unknown is very real. It's why God speaks to the topic more than three hundred times in the Bible.[36] God knew we would struggle with fear, so He equipped us with biblical tools to overcome that fear. He gave us His Word to speak truth over our fears.

What did John teach in 1 John 4:16?

_____

_____

Read 1 John 4:17–21.

Let's review the core truths we have learned:

God is love (1 John 4:16).

When we receive Jesus into our hearts as Lord and Savior, God seals us with His Spirit (Ephesians 1:13).

One fruit of God's Spirit is love (Galatians 5:22).

Through His Spirit, God plants His love in our hearts. As our faith matures, His love matures in us.

So, when John wrote in 1 John 4:17, "This is how love is made complete among us," or "By this, love is *perfected* with us" (NASB), he was specifically referencing how God's love works in us.

As we abide in God's love, His love "grows up" in us. The longer we walk with God, the deeper we go in His Word. The deeper we go in His Word, the more we understand and have the capability to understand His love and walk confidently in that love.

Read Matthew 17:5 and write the words spoken by the Voice out of the cloud. After you write those words; write them again but replace "My Son" with your name.

Do you know that you are God's beloved daughter?

Do you know that He loves you and is pleased with you?

Do you know you are His joy and delight?

Do you know you are the apple of His eye?

You are! And He loves you more than the stars in the heavens and the sands on the shores.

If we want to overcome fear, we must not only know these truths, we must believe them with all our hearts and walk confidently in them. How do we do this?

Reading the Word.

Learning the Word.

Digesting the Word.

Memorizing the Word.

Praying the Word.

We must allow God's Word to infiltrate every part of our being. Without truth reigning and ruling over our lives, we will be easily swayed by Satan's lies, entangled in his schemes, and crippled by his cunning.

In addition to God's love working in us to overcome our daily fears, 1 John 4:17 explains that God's love gives us a confidence and a boldness in the "day of judgment." Day of judgment refers to the time when all people will appear before God and be held accountable for their words and actions (Matthew 12:36; 16:27; Romans 14:10–12; 2 Corinthians 5:10).

If we know and believe we are loved by God; if we know and believe we are saved by the blood of Jesus; if we know and believe our names are engraved forever in the palm of God's hand, then we need not fear anything . . . even judgment day.

Why? Because we can trust a love that sacrificed His one and only Son for us. A love that willingly gave His life for ours.

Jesus took our place. Your sin and mine required a just payment. That payment was death, and Jesus paid it. He paid it all. God laid our sin on Jesus. And if that isn't enough, Jesus's gift keeps on giving because God also credited Jesus's righteousness, His right standing with God, to our spiritual account. The perfection and holiness of God Himself has become ours in Christ Jesus.

All who receive this gift by faith can stand boldly and confidently before the throne of God on judgment day. Jesus secured our place in God's family now and for all eternity!

And there's more!

Let us not forget God's promise in 1 John 3:2: "My loved ones, *we have been adopted into God's family; and* we are officially His children now" (The Voice).

On judgment day, our salvation will not be at issue. Christ paid that debt. It will only be about rewards and blessings for how we lived while on this earth. The judgment seat of Christ is where the Lord will judge believers by their works.

The word for "judgment seat" in the Greek is *bema*, meaning the place where the judges stood at the athletic games. If during the games, they saw an athlete break the rules, they immediately disqualified him. At the end of the games, the judges gave out rewards.

So how do we prepare for our appearance before the judgment seat of Christ? By living in alignment with John's teachings. Making Jesus Lord of our lives. Walking in the light. Walking in love. Walking in obedience to His Word. Loving others as He loves us. Oh, friend, we must be concerned more with *how we live* than about judging the lives of others.[37]

John returns to the topic with which he began: fear. First John 4:18 states there is no fear in love because God's perfect love casts out fear. When we receive, experience, and walk in the fullness of God's divine love, we need not fear His correction or judgment because we know God always acts in accordance with His sacrificial, grace-filled, mercy-driven, unconditional love. We can be absolutely assured of that because God is immutable . . . unchanging . . . the same yesterday, today, and forever.

We also need to remember the promise in 1 John 4:17, "because as He is, so also are we in this world" (NASB). Positionally, right now as you read these words, you are "as He is." God so closely identifies us with Christ— as members of His family—that our position in this world is like Jesus's exalted position in heaven. We have His blessings. His righteousness. His promises. His holiness.

Hold on to this truth: our Father deals with us just the same way He deals with Jesus, His one and only beloved Son. So how can we ever be afraid?

When we walk and live in the confidence of that kind of unconditional, extravagant, generous love, we can trust God with each coming day, even that final day when we meet Him face-to-face. On that final judgment day, we can lift our heads fearlessly, look deep into the eyes of the One we *know* is our friend and our Father, and trust whatever He decides. We need not fear . . . ever.

Read Romans 8:38–39 again. Personalize this passage and write it below. I encourage you to memorize it and hold it close to your heart.

_____

_____

_____

Glory! Get this, my friend. NOTHING in all creation, present or future, can come between us and God's love! We need never live imprisoned by fear and insecurity because God's faithfulness ensures we live every day enveloped in His love and girded with His confidence.

As Scripture says, "When struck by fear, I let go, depending *securely* on you *alone*" (Psalm 56:3 The Voice). Or, "Surely God is my salvation; I will trust and not be afraid. The LORD, the LORD himself, is my strength and my defense; he has become my salvation" (Isaiah 12:2).

Sweet friend, God is our protector. Our shield. Fear cannot touch us when we allow His Spirit to swell in all His fullness within us.

I'm going to share a couple more verses. But this time, let's personalize them:

Daughter of the One True God, I do not give you a spirit of fear. Fear is not from Me. I infuse you with My divine power; fill you with My unconditional, everlasting love, and equip you with a sound and stable mind. I implanted all of this in you through My Holy Spirit! (2 Timothy 1:7)

Daughter of the King, be strong and courageous! Never be afraid or discouraged because I am your God. I will never leave you or forsake you and will remain with you wherever you go. (Joshua 1:9)

Do you see now how God created you so that His love lives and comes alive in you, enabling you to combat your fears?

Friend, His love, especially as expressed through the promises in His Word, speaks to every one of our "conditional mights," every one of our "what ifs." When they arise, recognize them, capture them, and hurl them deep into the ocean of His love. Drown them with truth until you hear them no more.

God is the answer . . . the only answer . . . to all our fears.

John closes chapter four by again teaching us about loving others. He reminds us that we love only because God first loved us. God ignited a spark that continues to burn. And His Spirit continually kindles that flame so that we can pass it on to others.

What does 1 John 4:20 say about a person who says he loves God but hates his brother?

_____

_____

Note how the following verses reveal how we should love others.

♥ **Matthew 18:21–22**

_____

♥ **Luke 6:31**

_____

♥ **Luke 6:35**

_____

♥ **Galatians 6:2**

_____

♥ **Ephesians 4:2**

_____

♥ **Philippians 2:3–4**

_____

Did any of these Scriptures speak to your heart? If so, journal below what you heard from the Lord and determine one step you will take in response to what you heard. Invite God to help you take that first step.

_____

_____

_____

_____

_____

_____

_____

Apply It

Let's engage in a bit of self-reflection.

On a scale of 1 (not very important) to 10 (very important), rank the importance of the following to you:

People accept me for who I am. _____

I feel loved and significant. _____

When I make a mistake, others don't condemn me. _____

People value my opinion. _____

I'm included and invited to events, parties, and groups. _____

Now examine your rankings.

Do they give you any insight into your fears?

_____

_____

Could your answers influence your willingness to love others?

_____

_____

Prayerfully put your rankings before the Lord and invite Him to fill any void they may reveal with the unconditional, wild-and-crazy, amazing love He has for you.

Goodness, it seems nearly impossible to live up to the standard of God's love, doesn't it? On our own, it is. Loving God's way requires faith and the willingness to live in step with the leading of His Spirit . . . no matter how hard, how awkward, or how humbling.

And take heart, as you embark on loving others, that our God is patient. So very patient. Every step we take toward loving others is big in God's eyes. He simply wants to see us working toward that goal, just as parents like to see their children working toward goals they set for them. So be encouraged, sweet friend. Keep putting one foot in front of the other. Keep loving out of His reserve. Eventually, you will surprise yourself. Heart change will come. You will find yourself loving and forgiving people that you never thought possible!

Group Discussion Questions

1. This week we talked about walking in faith.

   a. Define faith.

   b. What does it look like to walk in faith?

   c. What keeps you from confidently walking in faith?

2. We have an enemy whose chief objective is to dismantle our faith piece by piece.

   a. Share tactics Satan has used to cripple your faith.

   b. What helps you fight back when you find yourself in a battle with Satan?

3. Read 1 John 4:4. John declared first *who* we are.

   a. Who are you?

   b. How does knowing your true identity affect what you think and believe about yourself?

   c. John tells us we are a "new creation." What freedom, maybe even victory, do you gain from knowing "the old has gone and the new has come" (2 Corinthians 5:17)?

4. Next John declared *what* we are.

   a. What are we?

   b. Romans 8:37 tells us that "*in all these things*, we are more than conquerors through him who loved us." What are "these things" in your life that keep you from confidently believing you are more than a conqueror?

c. Christ's victory on the cross guarantees you are an overcomer. In Him, you have the power to overcome every evil scheme of the enemy. What truths have you learned this week to help you not only know and believe this truth but also walk confidently in it?

5. Finally, John declared *why* we are overcomers.

a. Why are we overcomers?

b. The Spirit of God indwelling us equips and empowers us to flip-flop the pressure imbalance in our lives. Ensuring we live in the fullness of God's Spirit requires that we refresh and refill. We must continually "feed" the Spirit rather than our flesh (self). List some ways you can refresh and refill God's Spirit in you.

c. If you are experiencing a growth opportunity and feel pressure building, how can you specifically refill to help ensure the pressure subsides?

WEEK
FIVE

WALK IN VICTORY

PRAYER: *Precious Father, You have brought me such a long way. This is the last leg of my adventure with You. Thank You for all You have taught me these past weeks. Thank You for opening the eyes of my heart to receive and understand the wonderful things in Your Law. I long to continue my journey with You, Father. Draw me close. Open my ears so that I may hear Your voice calling, "This is the way, my beloved daughter, walk in it." Help me not to rush through my day without remembering all You sacrificed for me . . . without thanking You for the deep and abiding love You have for me. Even though my time in 1 John has ended, help me to continually turn my thoughts toward You so that I don't exclude You from my days. Father, capture my gaze and overwhelm my heart with Your love and Your presence. Lead me to open Your Word, and when I do speak, Lord, speak Your thoughts to me. Father, don't let me close this chapter and forget all that I have learned. Plant these words deep in my heart and enable them to take root. I give You my heart and hold nothing back. Help me to love others as You love. Instill in me a passion to pray like never before and trust that You hear my prayers and answer them in Your way and in Your time. Use me, Lord, to take what I have learned and do great things that will bring glory and honor and praise to You. Teach me to be a light in this dark world. Give me boldness and courage to live out my faith no matter the cost. I love You, Lord. Lead me down paths of righteousness; fill me with everlasting joy; use me, Lord; use me for Your glory! I ask this in Jesus's name. AMEN!*

Love Moves Us

MEMORY VERSE: *Whoever has the Son has life; whoever does not have the Son of God does not have life.* (1 John 5:12)

Children of God. Servants. Ambassadors. Stewards. Witnesses. Letters of Christ.

These are names Scripture gives to believers. Like a multifaceted precious stone, each name reveals a role we play in God's kingdom. Each role is valuable and contributes to the spiritual house God is building (1 Peter 2:5). Implicit in each name is a heart to love and serve others.

Yet, we live in a society where many live only for themselves. The mantra of our culture says do whatever it takes to get ahead. From Wall Street to Hollywood, the message is consistent. Cheat. Lie. Steal. Whatever it takes, do it.

But living for self goes beyond Hollywood and Wall Street. It hits home . . . often. When someone wrongs us, we retaliate. When someone hurts us, we harbor bitterness. When someone needs forgiveness, we withhold it. When we see someone in need, we ignore it.

This live-for-self message most notably manifests itself in social media. It might be the perfectly decorated homes we covet on Pinterest. The luxurious cars intentionally positioned during commercial breaks on our favorite shows. The pictures of extravagant vacations our friends share on Instagram. Each one tempting us to desire bigger and better. To splurge and live beyond our means.

Jesus commands us to live differently. To live a life not centered on self but centered on others.

♥ **His first commandment is to love _____ (Matthew 22:37).**

♥ **His second commandment is to love your _____ as _____ (Matthew 22:39).**

John wanted his audience to understand that the two go hand in hand. When we know and love God, when Jesus lives in our hearts, God's love will rule and reign in our hearts. That love pours out and is evidenced by how we live and treat others. We won't seek to be more, do more, and have more. We will seek, instead, to be ambassadors, servants, lovers of people.

How does John 13:34–35 speak to what we are talking about?

_____

_____

Digging Deeper

Read 1 John 5:1–3.

God's love leaves an indelible mark on our hearts because it's a distinctive love that, when allowed to blossom and mature, is proof of a changed life. His love becomes a driving force that nothing can contain.

Is there someone you know whose life oozes God's love? What is it about her that reveals God's love in all she says and does?

_____

_____

God equips us to live distinctively different lives. First, by eradicating our old self through Jesus's death on the cross. Second, by bestowing upon us a new self through His resurrection.

What does it look like to live distinctively different?

Reread 1 John 5:1.

In verse one, John makes clear that when we accept Jesus as our Lord and Savior, God adopts us into His family. God's role broadens from Creator to Abba Father. Our family expands from DNA blood brothers and sisters to blood-bought brothers and sisters in Christ. We have instant new family!

As an only child, I love this truth. But as a Bible study girl, I love it even more. You and me. We are sisters in Christ. We are family! And not just for our short time on this earth. We are friends for all eternity! How cool is that?!

And this love is not dependent on how lovable our people are. It springs from our paternity . . . from the identity of our Father . . . and the identity of our brother, Jesus.

So now, back to love. We express our appreciation for these abundant blessings most beautifully when we love others and live a life marked by love. Some may be lovable people . . . those are the easy ones to love. Some may be difficult people . . . those are the challenging ones to love. Some may be invisible people . . . those are the uncomfortable ones to love.

Who are the invisible? The disenfranchised. The voiceless. The forgotten. The rejected. The unpopular.

Think of a time in your life when you loved someone lovable, some-one challenging, and someone invisible. Now I have a bigger assign-ment. Take some time to examine how you expressed your love to each person, how it was received, and what God did with that love in your life and the life of the one to whom you showed love. Did one change or affect your life more than another? If so, how?

What did you learn about yourself by going through this exercise?

Reread 1 John 5:2–3.

Let's summarize what we have learned.

💜 We have been born of God.

💜 God loves us.

💜 We love God.

💜 We are a child of God.

💜 In Christ, we have blood-bought brothers and sisters in Christ.

Knowing these truths equips us to live loved and spill that love into this dark world.

How do we demonstrate this love (1 John 5:2–3)?

We best demonstrate our love for God not by our words but by our actions. Where love resides, a willingness to trust follows. We readily trust and follow someone whom we love and whom we know loves us.

Our family loves to visit Disney World, which has some of the greatest roller coasters in the world. My daughter, Lauren, has always loved to ride roller coasters, but neither of her parents do. So, when her brother, Bo, reached the approved height, she constantly begged him to join her. Harassed him when he didn't. She never gave up. Yet, no matter the size or speed of the rollercoaster, Lauren's invitation was met with the same emphatic no. I totally understood. Sister, you couldn't get me on a roller coaster for any amount of money. I don't like surprises. I don't like the unexpected. I don't like being tossed about like a tennis shoe in the dryer. And that's what roller coasters do. They're chock-full of unexpected twists and turns taken at an insane speed while holding the rider hostage in a tiny torture chamber.

Like mother, like son.

Well, the time came for Bo to go to an amusement park with his buddies, not his family. Upon arrival, the boys sprinted to the biggest, baddest, most terrifying (my opinion!) ride in the park. Bo lagged behind; he was in quite a quandary. I had predicted this, and he and I had talked beforehand how he would handle the invitation if it arose. I prayed before and during his outing because I knew what would happen if he said no. His friends would give him a hard time . . . for a long time.

But was I wrong. Something amazing happened that day at the park. Instead of taunting and teasing him, two of Bo's best buddies talked him through the ride. They rode first. Bo anxiously watched and waited. When his friends returned, they said, "Come on, Bo, you can do this." It was clear they weren't going to take no for an answer again. Hesitantly, he agreed. In between the hooting and hollering, they encouraged him at every twist and turn. And when it was over, Bo had conquered his fear of roller coasters. In fact, he went on to ride many more that day.

His story melted my heart. Their combination of firmness *and* kindness helped Bo overcome his fear. Why was he willing to go with his friends that day? Maybe because, unlike his sister, they patiently encouraged him. And because of that, he trusted them and was willing to take the risk.

Where there is love, there is a willingness and desire to serve, to participate, to step out in faith, to obey. I'm convinced that people don't care to hear our words about Jesus until they see the reality of Jesus on display in our lives. God's truth lived out through us is the best sermon we could ever preach.

We live love when we . . .

> show compassion,
>> pray with and for another,
>>> serve those in need,
>>>> give grace,
>>>>> encourage others,
>>>>>> and share our abundance.

Apply It

John closes this section with these words: "His [God's] commandments are not burdensome."

Here's how 1 John 5:3 reads in the Amplified Bible: "For the [true] love of God is this: that we do His commands [keep His ordinances and are mindful of His precepts and teaching]. And these orders of His are not irksome (burdensome, oppressive, or grievous)." And here's the same verse in The Message: "The proof that we love God comes when we keep his commandments and they are not at all troublesome."

The more God's love flourishes within us, the easier obedience becomes. It's called "joyful obedience." We joyfully obey because we trust God's every word, and we know His character. He is faithful (1 Corinthians 1:9). He is just (2 Thessalonians 1:6). He is good (Psalm 73:1). He wants only the best for us. He promises that His blessings follow obedience, and we want to be beneficiaries of that promise.

Of course, Jesus never promises that obedience will be easy. In fact, He tells His disciples, and us, quite the opposite. But what He does promise is that following and obeying Him is not burdensome to those who know and love Him. And if our load ever begins to feel burdensome or too heavy to bear, we need only take it back to Jesus, our burden-bearer.

Read Matthew 11:28–30, and then write it below. What does this Scripture mean to you with what you are carrying today?

_____

_____

_____

Read through the list right before this "Apply It" section on how we can best live out God's love. Choose one way you can share God's love with someone in your life. And then, do it . . . today!

Love Overcomes

MEMORY VERSE: *Whoever has the Son has life; whoever does not have the Son of God does not have life.* (1 John 5:12)

Monty and I began our marriage in a difficult place. Eleven months before we walked down the aisle, I was the victim of a horrific crime. Few knew the fear and despair shrouding my heart.

Intimacy was hard because it brought back terrible memories. I tried to be a "good" wife and make my husband happy. But I just couldn't.

Yet, I needed Monty. When fear consumed me, he was my safe place. Being home alone terrified me. So, when he chose to leave me to play basketball or go to dinner with friends, I pouted, whining and complaining that he wasn't putting me first.

This fractured our marriage. Days were hard and nights were long. Soon I began to imagine Monty looking elsewhere for the companionship he lacked with me. I demanded to know when and where he was at all times. When I couldn't get ahold of him, I panicked . . . my mind traveling to places and imagining things it shouldn't.

As jealous thoughts took root, they became a mental obsession that fed me lies. I knew these feelings were wrong. Even destructive. But I didn't know how to overcome them.

I felt my marriage, and my husband, slipping away. Completely at a loss to know what to do, I dropped to my knees and begged God to help me.

Thankfully, God made a way to release jealousy's grip on me—and it was through loving Him. As I came to know God more intimately, my jealousy subsided.

God opened my eyes to see Christ in a new way . . . as my Savior and my "first love." Until that time, I had found that love and security in Monty. I had confused love and need. I needed Monty so desperately that he became my savior. He was my defender and my protector from the evil in the world. I needed him more than anything else. If I was with him, I felt safe.

Monty sat on the throne of my heart, not God.

This, sister, is the perfect recipe for an unhealthy, destructive relationship. We should never "need" our husbands, our children, or anyone else more than Christ. Ironically, I was so afraid of losing Monty that I treated him in a way that could potentially have driven him away.

We should have only one Savior, and His name is Jesus.

We should have only one first love, and His name is Jesus.

Healing came. Jesus replaced Monty as my first love. Jesus is now my Defender, my Refuge and my Strong Tower. It was in Him and Him alone that I overcame all my fears. It was in Him and Him alone that I attained freedom and victory from all that held me captive.

This knowledge put my marriage in perspective. Monty became the gift God had given me on this earth to reveal His perfect love to me. As God took His rightful place on the throne of my heart, Monty took his rightful place too. Our marriage changed dramatically.

Of course, I never want to lose Monty, but I have come to know that I could and would be able to live without Him. He and my children are precious gifts God has given me.

Digging Deeper

Read 1 John 5:4–5.

In this passage, John speaks of how to be an overcomer . . . a victor who overcomes the world.

Do you own any clothes imprinted with the infamous Nike logo? Why did you buy it?

The brand?

The swoosh?

The "cool" factor?

Because LeBron James and Kevin Durant endorse it?

When you bought it, did you even know the meaning of the word *Nike*? I didn't.

Nike derives from the Greek word *nike* (NEE-kay), which means "victory." [38] Now that's a reason to buy sports gear, right? If I sport these shoes . . . this uniform . . . play with this basketball . . . I will experience victory. Well, probably not. But that's what the advertisers hope we'll believe.

Who is it that overcomes the world (1 John 5:4)?

_____

_____

What characterizes an overcomer? John contends it's the foundational belief that Jesus is the Son of God.

Read John 1:12; John 14:6; Acts 4:12; and 1 Corinthians 3:11. How do each of these verses add to our discussion?

_____

_____

_____

God's Word is clear. Any claim that advances the notion that people can be saved apart from faith in Jesus Christ is biblically untenable.

213

Remember when John spoke of this truth earlier in 1 John 2:22–23? Reread his words and write them below.

_____

_____

Hear this and never forget it. It is our faith in Jesus that allows us to overcome the world.

When we accept Jesus as our Lord, we receive two gifts:

1. A New Promise

"Through these [His divine power and our knowledge of Him] he has given us his very great and precious promises, so that through them you may participate in the divine nature, having escaped the corruption in the world caused by evil desires." (2 Peter 1:4)

2. A New Nature

"Therefore, if anyone is in Christ, the new creation has come: The old has gone, the new is here!" (2 Corinthians 5:17)

Through His divine power, God allows us to participate in His divine nature. Living fully in the power of our new nature guarantees we live victoriously.

You see, the world appeals to our old nature, but the Spirit appeals to our new nature. Inherent in the life of every believer is a battle between these natures. But when we are born of God, John tells us our new nature guarantees we will be an overcomer!

Hear this truth: You are an overcomer!

We claim this not because of anything we do or say. We claim it because of our identity. We are children of God. It is our faith in Jesus Christ, the Son of God, that gives us the victory. John 16:33 says, "I have told you these things, so that in me you may have peace. In this world, you will have trouble. But take heart! I have overcome the world."

Remember, "because as he is so also are we in this world" (1 John 4:17 ESV).

Pay close attention to this progression of biblical events.

💜 When Christ died, we died with Him (Romans 6:8).

💜 When Christ was buried, we were buried with Him (Romans 6:4).

💜 When Christ arose, we arose with Him (Romans 6:4).

💜 When Christ ascended into heaven, we ascended with Him and were seated with Him in the heavenly realms (Ephesians 2:6).

💜 When Christ returns, appearing in all His glory, we too shall appear with Him in glory (Colossians 3:4).

This is the position we talked about earlier . . . our position in Christ. Positionally, spiritually, we sit where Jesus sits.

Read Ephesians 1:20–22. Where does Jesus sit?

_____

_____

When we stand firm in this position, we share Christ's victory. Our authority is determined not by our earthly location but by where we stand in relation to Christ. Friend, Jesus came to destroy the works of the devil. By His death and resurrection, Jesus has defeated every enemy of God in the heavens, on the earth, and under the earth. And in the last days, God's greatest enemy, Satan, will meet his final doom.

Revelation 20:10 declares, "And the devil who had deceived them was cast into the lake of fire and sulfur, where the beast and the false prophet had already been thrown; and the _unholy_ trio will be tortured day and night throughout the ages" (The Voice).

On that day, Satan will no longer be a threat to anyone. Never. Ever. Again!

We may have hard days. Days we cry out as David did, "How long will you hide your face from me?" (Psalm 13:1). Days we feel we cannot put one foot in front of the other. Days we want to walk away from it all. But in those moments, we must

> REMEMBER and
>> STAND in
>>> WHO we are in Christ.

We are children of the One True God . . . the King of Kings, the Lord of Lords . . . the One who is all authority in heaven and on earth. Our unwavering belief in this truth guarantees that our faith will never fail. On hard days, speak these truths over your heart, mind, and circumstances again and again and again.

Apply It

Get ready, my friend. I'm taking you on a detour for a moment to another of John's writings, the book of Revelation. Please don't stop reading. I know what you are thinking. Revelation! It's too hard. I feel the same way. It's a book I always hesitated to teach because it intimidates me. But during my research for this study, I tackled parts of Revelation and learned so much. I can't wait to share what I learned with you!

Here are some truths we have discovered from 1 John:

♥ God delights in His children.

♥ His children are overcomers.

♥ God pours out blessings and makes great promises to those who are overcomers.

In John's letter to the seven churches in Revelation 2–3, we hear more about the special blessings Jesus promises to all overcomers.[39]

Read each passage (letter) and look for the promise(s) in the last verse(s) of each.

♥ Read Revelation 2:1–7, to the church in Ephesus. What is the promise?

_____

_____

♥ Read Revelation 2:8–11, to the church in Smyrna. What is the promise?

_____

_____

♥ Read Revelation 2:12–17, to the church in Pergamum. What is the promise?

_____

_____

♥ Read Revelation 2:18–29, to the church in Thyatira. What is the promise?

_____

_____

♥ Read Revelation 3:1–6, to the church in Sardis. What is the promise?

_____

_____

♥ Read Revelation 3:7–13, to the church in Philadelphia. What is the promise?

_____

_____

♥ Read Revelation 3:14–22, to the church in Laodicea. What is the promise?

_____

_____

Now let's go through them together.

Ephesus

The promise to the church in Ephesus is eternal life.

Smyrna

The promise to the church in Smyrna is that they will not die spiritually and eternally; they will not spend eternity in hell. It's the flip side of the first promise.

Pergamum

Jesus made two promises to the church in Pergamum. The first is God's provision for their needs (just as God provided tangibly through manna for His people in the desert). The second is admission into heaven (in that time, the "white stone" was given to victorious athletes in the games and served as an admission pass to a special celebration for the winners).

Thyatira

Jesus made two promises to the church in Thyatira. First, He gives the honor of ruling the nations with Him. Second is the gift of "the morning star." Friend, Jesus is the Morning Star (Revelation 22:16). So, Jesus is promising Himself in all His fullness!

Sardis

Jesus made a three-part promise to the church in Sardis. First, perfect holiness and purity. The blood of the Lamb washed their sins away. But one day He would free them from any sin that still entangled them. Second, their names would never be erased from the Lamb's book of life. In ancient times, if a citizen committed a heinous crime, the government might expunge his name from the registry, making him an outcast in the community. Jesus promised here that under no circumstance would a true believer's name ever be removed from the Lamb's book of life. And finally, Jesus promised to confess every believer's name before His Father in heaven!

Philadelphia

Jesus made three promises to the church in Philadelphia. First, stability and permanence. They would forever be a permanent part of His family . . . an integral, immovable part of His temple. Second, eternal security. Third, a permanent mark displaying to all the world that they are His beloved possession, members of His family for all eternity.

Laodicea

Jesus makes a spectacular promise to the church in Laodicea. He promises them the privilege of sitting with Him on His throne. He shares His Father's throne, and overcomers will share His throne and reign victoriously with Him forever and ever.

Do these promises sound familiar? They should. Throughout this study, we have talked about many of them. Promises that are ours in Christ Jesus.

Which of these promises gives you the most hope? Why?

_____

_____

1 John

What phrase precedes each of the promises (i.e., Revelation 2:7, 11, 17)? Why do you think Jesus began each promise with these words?

_____

_____

Friend, we are either *overcome by* our circumstances or we are *overcomers of* our circumstances. More simply said: We are either *overcome* or we are *overcomers*.

Let me say that again. We are either overcome or we are overcomers.

Which are you? Satan wants nothing more than for us to feel overwhelmed and overcome by our circumstances, our emotions, and the myriad of difficult trials that cross our paths in this life. Satan will use every weapon at his disposal to ensure such an outcome. But when you and I yield our lives to Christ, when we surrender our hearts and lives to Him, the evil one cannot hold us captive. God infuses us with a new nature, a new identity, a new empowerment, a new equipping.

We are overcomers, never again to be overcome by the world!

Jesus makes a promise in John 16:33 that we must never ever forget. He warns: *in the world, you will have tribulation.* Bad things will happen. Jobs will be lost. Sickness will come. Husbands will leave wives. Children will rebel. People will let us down. Disasters will occur. Death will steal a loved one.

But Jesus doesn't stop there. He goes on to say: *take courage.* The King James translates it, "Be of good cheer." Why? Because we are not alone. Jesus will never abandon us. He will never leave us or forsake us. He has already overcome each one of our circumstances. It's in Him alone we find the strength to endure. The hope to persevere. The courage to move on. The faith to believe.

Taking courage becomes easier the deeper in love we fall with Jesus. As God perfects His love in us, that love casts out fear. Confidence grows. As confidence grows, trust flourishes. Any fear that attempts to raise its ugly head evaporates when we speak His truth over that fear. We are overcomers!

Obedience becomes not only easier but also desirable. We long to please our Father. And this . . . this is the place where God pours out His blessings.

Are you overcome by a circumstance or circumstances in your life or are you an overcomer? If life overwhelms you at times, did something you read today provide insight as to why? What is one step you can take toward believing and walking in the truth that you are an overcomer?

_____

_____

_____

_____

Love Is Certain

> **MEMORY VERSE:** *Whoever has the Son has life; whoever does not have the Son of God does not have life.* (1 John 5:12)

hat do you *know* for sure . . . for certain . . . without a doubt? Perhaps the only thing all people know for certain is that we will die a physical death. Our bodies will plumb wear out!

Yet, we desperately want certainty, especially when it comes to finances, health, children, job security, and marriage. We want it so much that some dabble in fortune-telling and spiritism in search of that certainty. As Christians, Scripture forbids such activity. God's Word could not be clearer: "don't ever get involved in any divining, such as predicting fortunes, interpreting omens, sorcery, casting spells, or trying to contact ghosts, spirits, or the dead" (Deuteronomy 18:10–11 The Voice).

Instead, we find our hope in divine certainties—God-breathed truths and promises we can trust and know are true. Throughout this letter, John has hammered home a great number of these certainties.

God's children knowing and believing these truths has been his mission from chapter one, day one, when he opened with these words,

> *"That which was from the beginning, which we have heard, which we have seen with our eyes, which we have looked at and our hands have touched— this we proclaim concerning the Word of life. The life appeared; we have seen it and testify to it, and we proclaim to you the eternal life, which was with the Father and has appeared to us."* (1 John 1:1–2)

Knowing Jesus as Son of God and Savior of the world is the centerpiece of John's teachings. We find the word *know* nearly forty times throughout this letter and eight times in this chapter. If you've studied God's Word with me before, you know my thought on this. When God repeatedly uses a word or phrase, that word is significant, and we need to pay attention!

God scattered divine certainties about Jesus and His role in history throughout the Bible. They first appear in Genesis 3 in the Garden of Eden. They continue when God made this promise through Jacob: "The scepter will not depart from Judah; the ruler's staff will rest *securely* between his feet. Until the One comes to whom true royalty belongs, all people will *honor and* obey him" (Genesis 49:10 The Voice). In 2 Samuel, God promised David a Messianic King, "Your dynasty, your kingdom, will stand perpetually in My sight; *your descendants will rule continually*" (2 Samuel 7:16 The Voice). Psalm 2 reaffirms the promise of such a King, a King who is the Son of God!

If that isn't enough, the Old Testament prophesied specific details from Jesus's life thousands of years before He arrived. He would be born of a virgin (Isaiah 7:14); He would be born in Bethlehem (Micah 5:2); He would be called out of Egypt (Hosea 11:1); there would be one who would come to prepare the way for Him (Malachi 4:5–6); He would minister in Galilee (Isaiah 9:1–2); and He would be betrayed by a close friend (Psalm 41:9).

Even more compelling are the words of Psalm 22 and Isaiah 53, each foreshadowing the excruciating details of Jesus's persecution, crucifixion, and death.

Furthermore, John plainly states at the conclusion of his Gospel, "But these are written that you may believe that Jesus is the Messiah, the Son of God, and that by believing you may have life in his name" (John 20:31).

Every passage, from Old Testament to New, unmistakably points to Jesus Christ, each testifying to the fact that He is, without a doubt, the Son of God and our Messiah.

God desires a confident faith, and He provides us with ample evidence to secure it.

In this part of John's first letter, he delves into a few more truths upon which to base our confidence.

Digging Deeper

In 1 John 5:1–5, John emphasized the importance of trusting in Jesus, believing with all our hearts that He is the Son of God. He explained how believing this truth guarantees we can overcome any trial that arises.

Now John answers the question, *how* do we know Jesus is the Son of God? Let's remember his audience. Men and women who had been exposed to false teaching alleging Jesus was a liar. Labeling Him crazy. A mere man, denying His divinity and His divine power.

John flat out refuted these teachings by offering evidentiary proof that Jesus is God.

Read 1 John 5:6–9.

Name the three proofs (verse 6).

_____

_____

What do you think each symbolizes?

_____

_____

A foundational truth to our discussion today is this: Jesus's life did not begin in Mary's womb. In fact, John declared quite the opposite in the opening verses of his Gospel: "In the beginning the Word already existed. The Word was with God, and the Word was God. He existed in the beginning with God" (John 1:1–2 NLT).

Jesus is the Word. What John is telling us here is that Jesus was with God in Genesis 1:26, where we read, "Then God said, 'let _us_ make mankind in _our_ image, in _our_ likeness'" (emphasis added). God spoke in the plural. In the beginning, Jesus and God worked in tandem throughout the creative process.

And John explained further in John 1:14, "The Word became flesh and made his dwelling among us."

Make no mistake about it; Jesus willingly chose to come into this world. He left His glorious body and home in heaven and obediently took the form of a fetus, allowing His Father to implant Him in the secret place in Mary's womb.

Jesus left the perfection of heaven to dwell in our midst. His immaculate conception is a foundational belief in our faith.

John continued His testimony as to the legitimacy of Jesus's divinity by publicly declaring His credentials in 1 John 5:6: "This is the one who came by water and blood—Jesus Christ. He did not come by water only, but by water and blood." Jesus, the One who was, and is, and is to come, came by water and blood. Water and blood, the means by which Jesus would save us and heal us.

Let's study these evidentiary proofs a bit deeper.

First Evidentiary Proof: The Water

The water symbolizes Jesus's baptism.

Why was this significant to John's audience? Some of the Gnostics had taught that Jesus's divine nature came upon Him at His baptism, meaning He did not have it before that time. And they further asserted that His divine nature left Him at the crucifixion.

This teaching contradicts the miraculous acts accompanying Jesus's baptism. Jesus asked John the Baptist (not our author John) to cleanse Him through baptism. John obeyed, immersing Jesus in the Jordan River. His Father's voice proclaimed from heaven, for all to hear, words that distinctly revealed Jesus's divinity: "And a voice from heaven said, 'This is my Son, whom I love; with him I am well pleased'" (Matthew 3:17). And the moment Jesus emerged from the waters, the heavens opened, and the glory of the Lord descended like a dove and enveloped His Son, making a grand statement to all present that Jesus was God's Son, chosen by Him, to begin a ministry of reconciliation and redemption.

And why is the water still significant for us today?

What does water represent in everyday life? What happens when you use it?

_____

_____

Have you been baptized? What did the water symbolize to you?

_____

_____

John the Baptist's glorious encounter with Jesus came alive for me as I watched my daughter, Lauren, be baptized in the Jordan River on our trip to Israel. She confessed her sins in the same waters the New Testament believers stood as they confessed their sins. And I'll never forget the words she whispered following that sacred moment. Clothes dripping, tears of joy flowing, she said, "Mom, as I came up out of the water, it's like God showed me all my sins being carried down the river never to be seen again. Gone forever!" Hallelujah!

Don't miss this! Christ entered, and was baptized in, the same waters where thousands had made their confessions. And where many more thousands, like Lauren, will make their confessions. My girl's beautiful vision displayed the weight of this glorious moment in time . . . our Savior willingly entered our wretched world and immersed Himself in our sin-stained culture to wash our sins away and guarantee now and forever His forgiveness. His hope. His healing.

The significance of the word *water* also takes me to Hebrews 10:22 which says, "Let us draw near to God with a sincere heart and with the full assurance that faith brings, having our hearts sprinkled to cleanse us from a guilty conscience and having our bodies washed with pure water."

In the Old Testament, the Law required that the priests, before ministering before the Lord, wash their hands and feet at the laver, or basin, in the temple. Our God is a holy God; His holiness necessitated the priests cleanse themselves from anything that defiled their bodies. Washing at the laver accomplished that cleansing.

The water in the laver pointed to Jesus, the living Word of God.

Read John 15:3. What does it say about the Word?

_____

_____

We are born sinners, unclean to the depths of our souls. Water symbolizes spiritual cleansing. Like the Old Testament priests, our hearts and minds accumulate daily muck that needs to be washed in the water of His Word. And, returning to 1 John 1:9, when we confess our sins, "He is faithful and just and will forgive us our sins and purify us from all unrighteousness." We no longer need the laver because we have Jesus. His Word cleanses us from our sin so that we can confidently go before our holy God with a pure heart, a cleansed vessel able to receive all that He has for us.

Read Romans 12:2. What effect does the Word have on us?

_____

_____

Take a moment and thank Jesus for His most amazing gift.

Jesus, thank You for willingly breaking into history and our world to save us. For making a way for us to not only repent of our sins but also be forgiven of those sins and receive new life. Thank You for Your kindness and grace that has removed our sin as far as the east is from the west. We are the redeemed of the Lord. Help us to walk confidently in who and Whose we are! We ask this in Your holy and saving name. Amen.

Second Evidentiary Proof: The Blood

The blood represents Jesus's death.

Remember, John's goal was to refute the Gnostics' heretical teachings contending Jesus's divinity left Him before His suffering at the cross, alleging it was only Jesus, the human, who died. John sought to prove that Jesus was the Son of God not only at His baptism but also at His death.

Why do you think proving Jesus's divinity at the cross was so important?

_____

_____

Read Matthew 27:45–54 and note evidentiary proof that Jesus was God's Son, fully human and fully divine, upon taking His last breath.

_____

_____

Friend, the evidence God provided was *so* overwhelming that a Roman military soldier witnessing the execution cried out in horror, "Surely he was the Son of God!" (Matthew 27:54).

Let's look at the significance of the blood.

Read Leviticus 17:11 and Hebrews 9:22.

Guilt, and the condemning power of sin, stains our hearts and defiles our bodies, separating us from our Creator and Father. The only way back to our Father is through the shedding of blood. God established this in the very beginning when He shed blood for the animal skins that covered Adam and Eve, and when He required blood sacrifices from the Israelites to cover their sin (Genesis 3:21; Leviticus 17:11).

Old Testament law required that the Levitical priests offer sacrifices on a brazen altar made of acacia wood, covered in bronze. The fire burned round the clock as the priests presented their offerings and the offerings of God's people.

The brazen altar foreshadowed the cross, the place where Jesus offered His own blood as a once-and-for-all sacrifice for the forgiveness of sins. Christ's one-time sacrifice satisfied God's requirements for the Old Testament animal sacrifices. Never again would the blood of bulls, goats, and doves be used to cover sin. Jesus's blood fulfilled and superseded Old Testament rituals. Jesus is enough!

Jesus died in our place. He bore our punishment. He took away our sin . . . past, present, and future. Though we may suffer consequences for the sins we commit each day, Jesus bore the *eternal* penalty for those sins. His last words spoken from high atop the cross prove it: "It is finished" (John 19:30)!

He paid the penalty regardless of anything we have done, are now doing, or will do in the future. There is nothing more we need to do to receive the gift of His sacrifice. Nothing! If we confess our sin, He is faithful to forgive it.

Let's agree right now to stop living consumed by guilt; stop working to earn God's love; stop striving for "perfect." God paid the ultimate sacrifice for us—the life of His one and only Son. Instead, let's live a life of thankfulness for Jesus's sacrifice, walk confidently in His forgiveness, and live in the fullness of our redeemed life!

What do you need to let go of today to confidently walk in Jesus's forgiveness and live a redeemed life? Name one thing you can do to take a step foward and do it!

Third Evidentiary Proof: The Spirit

Finally, God gave His Spirit to bear witness to Christ.

Read John 15:26; 14:17. What characterizes the Spirit?

God's Spirit is Truth. God's Spirit was present in Jesus's conception (Matthew 1:18), descended on Him at His baptism (Matthew 3:16–17), empowered Him during His temptation (Luke 4:1), and remained with Him throughout His ministry, enabling Him to perform every miracle. Jesus did the will of His Father in tandem with the power of the Holy Spirit.

Near the end of His ministry, Jesus comforted His disciples with the promise that His Father would send His Spirit (John 14:16) to be with them forever. When we accept Jesus as our Lord and Savior, His Spirit serves as the guarantor that we are His children and beneficiaries of His riches and blessings. Because of the Holy Spirit's indwelling presence, we can walk confidently in our identity as children of God.

Additionally, the Spirit speaks to us and teaches us each time we meet God in His Word.

What does John 14:26 tell us about the role of the Holy Spirit in our lives? Have you ever experienced the activity of the Spirit in one of these roles? If yes, describe that time below. How did it impact your faith?

_____

_____

_____

_____

Deuteronomy 19:15 established that every "matter must be established by the testimony of two or three witnesses." The water, blood, and Spirit all convincingly testify that Jesus is the Son of God, fully human and fully divine. They are the witnesses God has provided. Can you think of any more reliable witnesses? Can you think of any more convincing proof?

Apply It

We find "water and blood" joined together again in John 19:34–35. This passage tells the account of the soldier who pierced Jesus's side with his sword, probably to make certain Jesus was dead. The instant the soldier thrust his sword into our Savior, blood and water poured forth from the wound. John is the only disciple who recorded this fact.

Was John the only eyewitness to it? Was he the only one touched by it? We'll never know this side of eternity. But I find it fascinating that John sees and records the flow of these spiritually life-giving fluids *after* Jesus poured out His life for us. After He spoke the words, "It is finished." Perhaps they serve as a forever sign that Jesus's assignment to walk among us as one of us was complete.

Take some time to be still and worship the One who willingly and lovingly shed His blood for you. Maybe you'll choose to listen to worship music. Maybe you'll choose to sit outside and listen to and experience the magnificence of God's creation around you. Maybe you'll choose to offer up a sacrifice of praise to your Redeemer. Whatever you choose, journal below what you feel, hear, and/or experience.

_____

_____

_____

_____

_____

_____

_____

_____

_____

Love Is Confident

MEMORY VERSE: *Whoever has the Son has life; whoever does not have the Son of God does not have life.* (1 John 5:12)

Can you believe you have hidden four Scriptures in your heart and are close to adding a fifth? I'm so proud of you! Don't give up. Memorize this last verse. Hide this truth in your heart to remind you of God's great promise that no matter what happens on this earth, you have the promise of eternity in your heart.

One day, your heart will swell as you pass into eternity and walk through the gates of your heavenly home.

Imagine with me . . .

I can hardly believe my eyes. All I've ever known is gone. Heaven and earth have passed away; the seas are gone. Everything is new! There, before me, is a holy city. It's the New Jerusalem, descending from heaven.

The glory of the Lord shines all about. The city is made of pure gold, yet it's as clear as glass. The great wall around the city, adorned with the most precious of jewels, glimmers unlike anything I've ever seen.

I see no street lights or lamps. But there's no need because the Light of the World illumines every corner of the city, forbidding darkness to enter.

The glory and grandeur of every nation is on display—people from around the world bringing glory and honor to the King of Kings and Lord of Lords.

Tears well up so thick. I can hardly take in what lies before me. A river of crystal-clear living water flows down from the throne of the Lamb. On each bank of the river stands the Tree of Life, firmly planted, bearing an abundance of plump, ripe fruit.

Surrounding me are worshipers, every race and every nation bowing before the throne of God and the Lamb of God. As I lift my eyes, I see my Creator and my Savior there before me. I'm in their presence. Awestruck wonder captivates my heart. I feel as if I can't breathe. I'd learned of God's glory. I had prayed often for a touch of His glory. But now, I can do nothing but fall on my face before His Shekinah glory and join the throngs of worshipers bowing down before Him, casting their crowns at His feet.

I hear a great voice, coming from the throne:

"The home of God is now with His people. He will live among them; they will be His people, and God Himself will be among them. The prophecies are fulfilled: He has wiped away every tear. No more death. No more mourning. No more pain. The first things have gone away."

And then I hear the One on the throne speak! A voice I have longed to hear announce to His creation:

"I am making ALL things new!"

Glory! Glory! It is all just as God said!

(Inspired by Revelation 21 and 22)

Oh, friend, I can't wait for that day!

John makes very clear near the end of Revelation, there is only one way we can *know* we will be present on that day. "Only those whose names are written in the Lamb's book of life *can enter*" (Revelation 21:27 The Voice).

Let's turn our attention to our next passage and read what John has to say on this topic.

$\mathcal{D}igging\ \mathcal{D}eeper$

Read 1 John 5:10–13.

On Day 3, we studied three witnesses to the fact that Jesus is the Son of God.

List the three witnesses (or evidentiary proofs).

_____

_____

Now John introduces another witness: the Word of God.

First John 5:13 says, "I write these things to you who believe in the name of the Son of God so that you may know that you have eternal life." John wrote his letters to provide further testimony about Jesus.

When presented with God's written Word, we have two choices. We can believe it or reject it. For those who reject the Word, Jesus issues a harsh warning: "Whoever is not with me is against me" (Matthew 12:30).

The one who believes God's testimony about His Son has God's Word living in their heart, and their belief in that Word guarantees their eternal life. John reinforces this truth in 1 John 5:10: "Whoever believes in the Son of God accepts this testimony. Whoever does not believe God has made him out to be a liar, because they have not believed the testimony God has given about his Son."

John makes clear that to deny Jesus is who God said He is, to refuse to believe the testimony God has given about His Son, renders God a liar and is the highest form of blasphemy. Blasphemy is showing great irreverence, contempt, or disrespect for God.

Read 1 John 5:12. Recognize it? Write it below.

_____

_____

The NASB rendering says, "He who has the Son has *the* life; he who does not have the Son of God does not have *the* life" (emphasis added). Did you notice that it's not just "life" but *"the* life"? It's not life in general or a good life. It is *the* life that is found only in the life-giving blood of Jesus Christ. Without the shedding of Jesus's blood, there is no life beyond this world. We would die in our sin and spend eternity separated from our Creator. But with the shedding of blood, we die to self and are raised up into a new life. Our new life allows us to spend eternity in the heavenly places in the presence of our Creator and Savior. Hallelujah! Can I hear an Amen?

Read John 1:12–13. How does this passage contribute to our discussion?

_____

_____

Oh, friend, you know the best part about this new life? We don't have to wait for it. It's not limited to what we receive upon our physical death. It is a present possession and begins the moment we invite Jesus into our hearts as our Savior. We don't have to work for it because it's already ours. We don't need to worry about it because it is guaranteed by the cross and the seal of God's Spirit. And once it is ours, no one and nothing can take it away (John 10:28)!

Our rebirth changes us from the inside out! The Holy Spirit works in and through us to rearrange our insides . . . our speech, our behavior, our attitudes, our desires, our motives, our emotions.

Before we move on, have you experienced this new life in Christ? Have you invited Jesus to be your Savior and Lord? If you haven't, it's not too late. God is waiting to give you a fresh start, to bring you into new life in Him. I would love to come alongside you in this decision. Pray this prayer today.

Lord, I confess that I have sinned against You, and I ask You to forgive me. I'm sorry that my sin has hurt You and other people in my life. I acknowledge that I could never earn salvation by my good works, but I come to You and trust in what Jesus did for me on the cross. I believe that You love me and that Jesus died and rose again so that I can be forgiven and come to know You. I ask You to come into my heart and be Lord of my life. I trust You with everything, and I thank You for loving me so much that I can know You here on earth and spend the rest of eternity with You in heaven. In Jesus's name, Amen.

If you prayed this prayer, congratulations! You are now a daughter of the One True God! Angels in heaven are celebrating because of your decision! Please share your step of faith with someone so that they can come alongside you and help you grow in your walk with Jesus.

If you prayed this prayer, write any thoughts or feelings you have below.

_____

_____

Read 1 John 5:14–15. What confidence do we have in prayer?

_____

_____

John moved from the Word to prayer. Prayer is the key that unlocks God's heavenly storehouse filled to overflowing with heavenly treasures and resources. As the author of Hebrews says about prayer, "Let us step boldly to the throne of grace, where we can find mercy and grace to help when we need it most" (Hebrews 4:16 The Voice).

We are to pray confidently. Boldly. We have that right and privilege because we are sons and daughters of the One True God. Through Jesus,

God has given us full access to talk with Him about anything and everything. Nothing is off limits.

John tells us that when we pray, to pray boldly because God hears us. The word *hear* derives from the Greek *akouo*, which in this context means more than God merely hearing the words we speak. The use of this particular word signifies that when God hears our prayers, He will *answer* our prayer.

But it's not a blank-check answer.

What qualifying words do you see in 1 John 5:14?

_____

_____

John qualified his statement with an "if." We must ask "according to his will."

What do these qualifying words mean to you?

_____

_____

God invites us to pray. Teaches us how to pray. But God also lays down some conditions for prayer.

Our Identity

We must be a child of God.

God promises to hear the prayers *of His children* (1 John 5:14).

Pure Heart

We must have clean hearts.

Unconfessed sin hinders our prayer life. It places a serious obstacle between our heart and God's heart. Psalm 66:18 says, "If I entertain evil in my heart, the Lord will not hear me" (The Voice). If we harbor sin (anger, unforgiveness, bitterness, unbelief, rage, etc.) in our hearts, we must settle that matter with God and with the other person (where possible) before we go to our Lord in prayer (Matthew 5:23–25). Broken relationships negatively affect, and even interrupt, our fellowship with God. God expects confession and reconciliation.

Abide in Christ

We must abide in Christ.

Jesus gave the disciples a few jaw-dropping promises. In Matthew 7:7, he says, "Ask and it will be given to you." And in Matthew 21:22, "If you believe, you will receive whatever you ask for in prayer."

But He qualified His promises with these words: "*If* you abide in Me, and My words abide in you, ask whatever you wish, and it will be done for you" (John 15:7 NASB, emphasis added).

Abiding is necessary because it's not our words that hold the power in prayer. It's His Word.

Let me say that again. It's not *our* words that hold the power in prayer. It's His Word. We must spend quality time with Jesus. Sitting at His feet. Reading His Word. Listening for His voice. Soaking in His presence.

It's also important for us to understand that answered prayer is not conditioned on the faithfulness or goodness of the one who *says* the prayers but the faithfulness and goodness of the One who *hears* the prayers.

When we allow our hearts to marinate in God's Word, it will eventually spill over into our prayers. We begin to pray not only our words but God's Word. Words that reflect His will. Our prayers change. They will align with God's will because His Word reflects His will.

Friend, you probably know this by now. But let's say it one more time. The goal of prayer is not to manipulate God to accomplish our will but to align our will with His. To align our hearts with His so we can accomplish His kingdom purposes on this earth.

1 John

Pray in Jesus's Name

Read John 14:13–14. What does this passage teach us about prayer?

_____

_____

To pray in Jesus's name is to pray consistent with His character and to pray as He prayed.

The disciples walked alongside Jesus for three years. They heard authority in His prayers. They experienced power through His prayers. They witnessed God working miracles through His prayers.

In response to what they saw, they asked Jesus how to pray. Jesus responded in Luke 11:1–4. Rather than giving them a long lecture on prayer, Jesus gave them a recipe. A model by which they could fashion their prayers. I memorized it as a child. I bet many of you have as well. But I've always struggled with how to make it my own.

Then I had the pleasure of participating in a conference call with the amazing pastor and teacher Max Lucado. He shared how he transformed Jesus's model prayer into a simple, easy-to-remember "pocket prayer."

> *Father,*
> *You are good.*
> *I need help. Heal me and forgive me.*
> *They need help.*
> *Thank you.*
> *In Jesus' name, amen.* [40]

His pocket prayer transforms this formula in to a comfortable conversation with God. First, he calls out to his Abba Father. Second, he offers words of praise. Next, he identifies where he needs help and brings it to the One he trusts and leaves it with Him. He cries out for healing and forgiveness. Then, he prays for those around him and around the world in need. Finally, He closes his prayer expressing thankfulness and praying in Jesus's name.

I love these one-word reminders:

- ♥ Worship (You are good).

- ♥ Trust (I need help).

- ♥ Compassion (they need help).

- ♥ Gratitude (thank you).

Mr. Lucado identifies each of the above words as prayer strengths. I may feel more comfortable praying in one prayer strength and you in another.

Considering your prayer life, which one of the four do you think is your prayer strength, and why?

_____

_____

If you want to learn more, visit Mr. Lucado's *Before Amen* website at BeforeAmen.com.[41]

Apply It

We must know God's Word to pray God's will. Our prayers pour forth from what we store in our hearts.

Over the past weeks, we have been memorizing God's Word. Hiding it in our hearts. Creating within each of our hearts a rich treasury of God's truths and promises. We now have the tools necessary to pray with great confidence that God's *will* be done in and through our prayers.

And know this. God may not answer immediately, but we have His promise in His Word that He will answer. It may be instantly. It may be gradually. And sometimes, it may not be till we get to the other side of eternity.

1 John

Read Hebrews 11:1. How does this verse speak to what we are studying about answered prayer?

_____

_____

Friend, if you are waiting on answered prayer, trust Jesus at His Word. Be patient in the "wait" room. The One upon whom you are waiting is trustworthy!

Take a few minutes to personalize and write your own pocket prayer.

_____

_____

_____

_____

_____

John's Concluding Thoughts

MEMORY VERSE: *Whoever has the Son has life; whoever does not have the Son of God does not have life.* (1 John 5:12)

We made it! We have reached the end of our journey together. How I wish I could hug each one of you right now and spend time celebrating our achievement. There are many ways you could have spent the past five weeks, and you chose to invest them on this journey with the disciple Jesus loves.

John's letter has demanded much of us, but you have not let up. You have persevered. You have been faithful. I'm so proud of what you have accomplished! And, be assured of this, God will richly bless your faithfulness.

We close our lesson today with some difficult words from John. Words with which I have struggled, praying and asking God for understanding. As we seek to decipher these verses and chew on them together, please don't be frustrated. Scholars and theologians alike are challenged by these verses and debate their meaning.

If great theologians can't understand them, why should we even try? Because God chose to include them in His Holy Scripture. That alone makes them important. He tells us in His Word that His ways are higher than our ways and His thoughts higher than ours (Isaiah 55:9).

So, stick with me as we study the closing words of 1 John.

Read Romans 11:33–36 and Job 38, 39, and 40:1–5 (where God answers Job's questions about why so much tragedy has come upon him).

What was Job's response to God's answer (40:3–5).

_____

_____

What fills your heart after reading these passages? Note your thoughts below.

_____

_____

An overarching truth for our lesson today is the sovereignty of God. This is a big word that means *nothing happens in the universe that is outside of God's authority and influence.* He is the ultimate source of all power, authority, and everything that exists (Romans 11:33; Colossians 1:16; Revelation 21:6). His methods, His means, His judgments are beyond tracing out, beyond anything we can fully comprehend.

In exercising His sovereignty, God is not arbitrary. He is intentional. He is ordered. He governs the universe and our lives with perfect wisdom, perfect justice, and perfect love. We must never forget these truths. N.E.V.E.R. Especially when we wrestle with discerning His Word.

When we don't understand a verse or a passage, we must never give up. Second Timothy 3:16 says, "All Scripture is God-breathed and is useful for teaching, rebuking, correcting and training in righteousness." God sent His Word for us. He wants us to understand it, so He gave us His Holy Spirit to help interpret it.

God said to Jeremiah, "Call to me and I will answer you and tell you great and unsearchable things you do not know" (Jeremiah 33:3). That same promise is for us. When we seek understanding, God will tell us unsearchable things we do not know. Sometimes God will give us full revelation and understanding, and sometimes we will need to walk in trust. His Spirit will lead us to which place we should land.

Keep these truths in mind as we chew on two meaty verses in 1 John 5:16–17.

Let me pray for us before we begin.

Heavenly Father, we love Your Word. We desperately want to know You better. Thank You for all You have taught us on our journey with John. As we close our study today, open our minds as we open Your Word. Reveal to us the unsearchable things we do not know. Grant us wisdom. Grant us a discerning spirit. Give us understanding beyond our years. We know You are able. We ask this in Jesus's name. Amen.

Digging Deeper

Read 1 John 5:16–21. Now reread verses 16 and 17.

These two verses will be the focus of our next discussion.

As we begin, remember a few verses earlier John emphasized boldness in prayer. Now he develops the topic of prayer a bit further, addressing intercessory prayer—praying for others. It's a good thing, right? We are called to pray for one another throughout Scripture. But John gets very specific here.

1 John

Before we bring in scholarly commentaries, read verses 16 and 17 again and prayerfully ask the Lord for understanding as to their meaning. Journal your thoughts below.

_____

_____

_____

John expounds on verses 14 and 15 as he probes deeper into the topic of praying for one another. He speaks specifically of prayers offered on behalf of those we know and love and who are struggling with sin.

Before we move on, we need to return to the topic of sin.

We all sin. None of us is perfect.

We studied sin in Week 3. Do you remember the distinction John made? The issue with God is the *practice* of sinning. John taught that no one born of God *practices* sin. It is habitual sin—an unrepentant state of continual, intentional sin—that brings down the full wrath of God.

We face enemies every day that draw us into sin. Satan is a formidable enemy who knows our vulnerabilities. He relentlessly feeds lies and temptations into those fragile places. He prowls around during times of weakness, doubt, and suffering (1 Peter 5:8). God's Word warns us to continually be on alert for his slithering presence among us.

Our tendency to sin was birthed in the garden with Adam and Eve. Their fallen nature is ours. Because of original sin, we are born with a bent toward selfishness. It's not something we learn; it's the natural inclination of our fallen nature. Our emotions and human desires long to be satisfied in the here and now. We want our way, and we want it now. This creates the perfect storm for us to fall prey to the desires of the flesh, the desires of the eye, and the pride of life, as did Adam and Eve.

The one who repeatedly falls prey to sin—the one who practices sin without remorse—proves that Satan, not God, is the lord of their life. And our holy God will only withstand rebellion and wickedness for so long. He reaches a point where He says no more.

Scripture teaches that there are certain acts of disobedience and rebellion that keep us from entering the kingdom of God.

Read 1 Corinthians 6:9–10. What does this passage teach about those who will not inherit the kingdom of heaven?

_____

_____

Read 1 Corinthians 6:11. What truth follows the verses above?

_____

_____

Read Mark 3:28–30. What hard truth do you glean from Jesus's words in this passage? What are your thoughts concerning His words?

_____

_____

Friend, I find such great comfort in Jesus's words that sins and blasphemies against God and man are open to God's gracious forgiveness. But there is one exception.

What is that exception?

_____

_____

Blasphemies against the Holy Spirit in this context refers to an *attitude* (not an isolated act or declaration) of defiant hostility toward God. An attitude that rejects His saving grace and the Spirit-empowered person and work of Jesus. As John taught us earlier, it is a person's preference for darkness even though they have been exposed to light (1 John 1:6; John 3:19).

1 John

Read John 3:19–21. Write this passage in your own words.

_____

_____

John and other New Testament writers contend that such a persistent attitude of willful unbelief can become so deeply engrained in an individual's heart that repentance and forgiveness, both mediated by God's Spirit, become impossible. And it is this attitude that John addresses here. Such a person is guilty (*enochos*, "liable to, in the grasp") of an eternal sin (the ultimate sin because it remains forever unforgiven).[42] Matthew 12:32 says, "Anyone who speaks a word against the Son of Man will be forgiven, but anyone who speaks against the Holy Spirit will not be forgiven, either in this age or in the age to come."

We find examples throughout Scripture of people dying because of their persistent defiance of God.

In Leviticus 10, two of the sons of Aaron, the priest and brother of Moses, died because they deliberately disobeyed God, abusing their office as priests in a flagrant act of disrespect (verses 1–2).

Another Levite, Korah, and his clan led a mini rebellion against God and Moses because Korah hungered for greater power, prestige, and privileges than he had been granted. As punishment for their wicked and rebellious hearts, the Lord caused the ground under the men's homes to split open and the earth to swallow not only them but also their households, their followers, and all their possessions (Numbers 16:31–33).

In Joshua's time, Achan and his family lost their lives by stoning when Achan pilfered plunder from the battle against Jericho in direct disobedience to God's explicit command to destroy everything connected to the city (Joshua 7). God saw Achan's heart and knew his sin was not simply a desire for the booty. God saw indifference to the evil and idolatry that defined Jericho and wanted to ensure Achan's sin was fully and completely purged from Israel.

And God's displeasure with this kind of defiance is not limited to the Old Testament.

Read Acts 5:1–11. What happened here?

_____

_____

_____

In another instance, some believers in Corinth died because they acted in an unworthy manner while taking the Lord's Supper (1 Corinthians 11:23–30).

And of course, Judas Iscariot's betrayal of Jesus also proves the reality that sometimes the consequence of defiance and rebellion against God may be death.[43]

Regarding this topic, Warren Wiersbe wrote, "If a believer does not judge, confess, and forsake sin, God must chasten him. This process is described in Hebrews 12:1–13, which suggests that a person who does not subject himself to the Father will not live (v. 9). In other words, first God 'spanks' his rebellious children, and if they do not yield to His will, He may remove them from the world lest their disobedience lead others astray and bring further disgrace to His name."[44]

Wiersbe concluded with the notion that the "sin unto death" is not one specific sin. Rather, it is a specific type of sin—it is the sort of sin that leads to death. With Aaron's sons, Nadab and Abihu, it was deliberately disobeying God's commands regarding the priesthood. With Achan, it was covetousness, desiring what was not his to have. With Ananias and Sapphira, it was greed, hypocrisy, and lying to the Holy Spirit.

Let's return to 1 John 5:14–15 (read it again if you need to) to connect the lessons above to John's words in verse 14. John wrote that when we see a sister or brother sinning, no matter the sin, we should pray for them. We pray with the hope that they will turn back to God with true repentance and reestablish fellowship with Him.

But, if while we are praying, we sense the person for whom we are praying might have entered that place of blasphemy or a sin leading to death, we must seek God's will regarding our prayer.

Let's be clear. John doesn't tell us *not* to pray.

Read 1 John 5:16 again carefully and write your understanding of John's instructions when we are praying for a person under these circumstances.

_____

_____

My understanding is that John's words don't forbid prayer, even in the most egregious situations. He recognizes the lack of certainty, but indicates that in such situations we should submit our prayer to the will of God. We should listen for His voice and trust what we hear. God is always the ultimate judge.

My conclusion: when in doubt, P.R.A.Y!

Now, let's move on to the final verses of John's letter.

Read 1 John 5:18–21.

I find great comfort in the next two verses, 1 John 5:18–19. As saved children of God, we can know with full assurance that the Good Shepherd watches over us and protects us. The evil one cannot touch us. This word *touch* in the Greek means "attach oneself to."[45]

Embrace this truth, my friend. Satan cannot touch us! He cannot lay hold of us or fasten his grip on us. We have been rescued from darkness and brought into God's marvelous light! Oh, he can tempt us, lie to us, and harass us, but he has absolutely no claim or power over us. We are anchored to the One True God.

Read these beautiful words from Hebrews 6:18–20:

"Therefore, we who have fled to him for refuge can have great confidence as we hold to the hope that lies before us. This hope is a strong and trustworthy anchor for our souls. It leads us through the curtain into God's

inner sanctuary. Jesus has already gone in there for us. He has become our eternal High Priest in the order of Melchizedek" (NLT).

Now read the same passage in the Amplified Bible:

"We who have fled [to Him] for refuge would have strong encouragement and indwelling strength to hold tightly to the hope set before us. This hope [this confident assurance] we have as an anchor of the soul [it cannot slip and it cannot break down under whatever pressure bears upon it]—a safe and steadfast hope that enters within the veil [of the heavenly temple, that most Holy Place in which the very presence of God dwells], where Jesus has entered [in advance] as a forerunner for us, having become a High Priest forever according to the order of Melchizedek."

Jesus will not fail His redeemed. We are His redeemed! You are His redeemed!

And although we live in this world that is temporarily under the control of the evil one, we need not fear because we belong to God.

Read John 15:18–19; 17:12–19; Philippians 3:20; and 1 Peter 2:9–12. How do each of these passages encourage you?

_____

_____

John closes his beautiful letter by bringing us full-circle back to Jesus coming as the Word of Life (1 John 1:1). In 1 John 5:20–21, he reminds us Jesus "has come." And the present tense of this verb, *heko*, indicates it is not a one-time occurrence.[46] Jesus has come and is still present.

Jesus came as a Son and remains with us as Immanuel, God with Us, through the living, breathing presence of God's Holy Spirit.

It's the Spirit who gives us understanding so that we may know our Father in heaven and His one and only Son. Three distinct beings, yet one God. The Trinity. Father, Son, and Holy Spirit. It's a beautiful mystery that we will never fully fathom.

Why did John close this way? Providing even more evidentiary proof? He had one false teaching left to address. The teaching alleging that a person had to belong to a special "inner circle" to obtain spiritual knowledge.

John responded with an emphatic no! Any believer in Jesus can ascertain God's truth through the power of the Holy Spirit living within them. We *know* Him who is true. We are *in* Him who is true. We are *empowered by* Him who is true.

We too have the real thing! Real means it's an original, not a copy. It's authentic. Not an imitation.

I'm a huge Coca-Cola fan! No Pepsi to be found in this girl's house. You are probably familiar with their memorable tag line since 1969: "It's the Real Thing." Coke is the original. And all copies are just that . . . copies. Counterfeits. They lack the ingredients in the super-secret recipe locked safely in a vault at the World of Coca-Cola in Atlanta that make Coke the drink so many, like me, savor.

Friend, we have the real thing in Jesus. He is the Original. And there is no other!

So, let's heed John's final warning to guard ourselves from idols. Let's be on alert for anything that captivates our hearts more than our Jesus; anything we enthrone in our hearts above God. They are all idols!

Proverbs 4:23 says it all: "Guard your heart above all else, for it determines the course of your life" (NLT).

How can we best guard our hearts and protect them from idols?

_____

_____

Do any idols come to your mind as we close our lesson today? Take some time and surrender them to the Lord in prayer. Take steps to put into practice your answer above.

This has truly been one of my favorite, yet most challenging studies. As I ponder what I have gleaned through these five chapters of 1 John, I've discovered God's beautiful design for His beloved. She is a woman who . . .

♥ lives in the Light

♥ knows, loves, and obeys her Father's Word

♥ lives fully loved by God

♥ loves others as she is loved

♥ knows and boldly speaks truth

The question I now ask myself is, do I faithfully and consistently live in this grand design for my life?

Most definitely, no. I try, but my bent toward self raises its ugly head more than I realize and more than it should. But I'm working on it daily. It's challenging, but not impossible. And I'm especially encouraged because God created us in His image. He patterned us after Himself. We have our Father's DNA.

We have the *mind* of Christ.

We have the *heart* of Christ.

We have the *will* of Christ.

The icing on the cake. We have God's Holy Spirit indwelling us. If we humbly allow the Holy Spirit to do His work, He will strip away self and impart more and more of Himself in our soul . . . our personality . . . our thoughts, feelings, conscience, and will.

It's when we move to the rhythm of self that we cannot walk in the beauty of God's design and who He created us to be. Self is all about independence and individuality. God created us for something so much greater.

Will you celebrate with me today God's beautiful design . . . who we are and what we possess as blood-bought children of the One True God?

Hear the truth, my friend: we have it all.

We have it all.

We not only possess the mind of Christ, but we have a *Spirit-controlled mind* that enables us to walk in the Light, to know and understand the deep things of God, the truths and promises in His Word, the things that an unsaved man or woman cannot know.

We not only possess the heart of Christ, but we have a *Spirit-controlled heart* that enables us to love everyone, even those who hurt us, betray us, or just plain annoy us. Even those we love on the days when we're mad as fire at them.

We not only possess the will of Christ, but we have a *Spirit-controlled will* that enables us to walk in joyful obedience to what we hear and boldly speak the truth we know.

Friend, leave this study fully confident that you are a daughter of the One True God, bought at a high price and treasured beyond your wildest imagination. May God's joy and peace fill and overflow as you daily walk in fellowship with your Savior and Redeemer, living your life in the abundance He promises . . . walking in the light of His love, mercy, and grace.

And on days when this seems impossible. On days when walking in the Light, walking in obedience, believing wholeheartedly, loving unconditionally seems impossible, pour out your heart to Jesus. He can take it. Your words will not go unheard. Your tears will not go unseen. He sees you. He knows you. He loves you. He created you. He is waiting for you.

The following is a proclamation from my heart to yours. As we end our time together, find a quiet place to be with your Abba Father and speak these words over your heart.

Jesus, I will not give in to self today.

Jesus, I align my heart afresh with Yours today.

Jesus, in You I can change my attitude.

Jesus, in You I can emerge from this dark place and walk boldly into the Light.

Jesus, in You I can believe this hard truth and claim it to combat the lies of the evil one.

Jesus, in You I can obey, even though everything in me wants to retaliate and punish.

Jesus, in You I can love, even though there is nothing lovable in this other person right now.

Jesus, in You I will stand strong and overcome because I am Your Beloved. I am Your blood-bought baby girl.

Jesus, in You I will boldly stand up for truth even though it may mean persecution and rejection.

Jesus, today I will listen for Your voice. I will position my heart so that I will follow where You lead.

I love You, Jesus. I ask all this in Your Holy Name. Amen.

Group Discussion Questions

1. John placed incredible significance on the fact that he and the other disciples were eyewitnesses to the words and stories he wrote in 1 John. Does knowing this affect your belief and/or confidence in what we studied? If so, how?

2. John wrote the words *know this* more than thirty times so that we would know what we believe, have confidence in what we believe, and live out what we believe.

   a. What truth or promise do you know with confidence now that you didn't know before you started this study?

   b. In what truth or promise have you gained confidence to live out that you did not have before?

3. John warned us to keep ourselves from idols.

   a. What idol is battling for first place in your life?

   b. What truths have you learned to help you dethrone your idol?

4. It's my heart's desire this study brought you to a place of deeper abiding in God's love . . . to truly understand, walk confidently in, and live out God's unconditional, extravagant, lavish love. It's a love He destined you for. Share one way God has intimately spoken to you and transformed your heart as you've met Him in the pages of 1 John.

✻ Endnotes ✻

1 According to the New American Standard Bible note (page 2216), scholars believe John wrote 1 John from Ephesus and circulated it among the churches in Asia.

2 Lawrence O. Richards, *The Teacher's Commentary* (Wheaton, IL: Victor Books, 1987), 1050.

3 *Strong's Expanded and Exhaustive Concordance, Red Letter Edition* (Nashville: Thomas Nelson, 2001).

4 www.dictionary.com.

5 www.bible-history.com/faussets/F/Fuller/.

6 www.keyway.ca/htm2003/20030821.htm.

7 *Strong's Expanded and Exhaustive Concordance, Red Letter Edition.*

8 Richards, *The Teacher's Commentary*, 1052.

9 David Jeremiah, *Living in the Light: Studies in First John* (San Diego: Turning Point, 2009), 39.

10 Jeremiah, *Living in the Light*, 40.

11 Richards, *The Teacher's Commentary*, 1053.

12 Warren W. Wiersbe, *The Bible Exposition Commentary*, 1 John 2:7–11 (Wheaton, IL: Victor Books, 1996).

13 *Strong's Expanded and Exhaustive Concordance, Red Letter Edition.*

14 Wiersbe, *The Bible Exposition Commentary*, 1 John 2:9–11.

15 *Strong's Expanded and Exhaustive Concordance, Red Letter Edition*, 2889.

16 K. S. Wuest, *Wuest's Word Studies from the Greek New Testament: For the English Reader*, 1 John 2:15–17 (Grand Rapids: Eerdmans, 1997).

17 Read more at www.songlyrics.com/mandisa/overcomer-lyrics/#YJcuC6Ub PvarMfIc.99.

18 Wuest, *Wuest's Word Studies from the Greek New Testament*, 1 John 2:18.

19 *Strong's Expanded and Exhaustive Concordance, Red Letter Edition*, 500.

20 John MacArthur, *MacArthur New Testament Commentary*, 1–3 John (Chicago: Moody, 2007), 114.

21 *The New Strong's Expanded Exhaustive Concordance of the Bible, Greek Dictionary of the New Testament*, #265 (Nashville: Thomas Nelson, 2001).

22   Ibid., #458.

23   *Strong's Expanded and Exhaustive Concordance, Red Letter Edition*, 3089.

24   Wiersbe, *Bible Exposition Commentary*.

25   Ibid.

26   Richards, *The Teacher's Commentary*, John 1 and John 3:11–12, quoting from *The Dictionary of New Testament Theology*.

27   MacArthur, *MacArthur New Testament Commentary*, 1–3 John, 132–133.

28   Ibid.

29   https://www.youtube.com/watch?v=a7QQGPvlIkc, "Jesus Paid It All."

30   John A. Martin, in John F. Walvoord and Roy B. Zuck (eds.), *The Bible Knowledge Commentary: An Exposition of the Scriptures*, Luke 10:25–37 (Wheaton, IL: Victor Books, 1985).

31   Wiersbe, *The Bible Exposition Commentary*, Luke 10:25–37.

32   *The Beloved Disciple's Memoirs and Letters*, Kindred Publications.

33   *The New Strong's Expanded Exhaustive Concordance, #27.*

34   MacArthur, *MacArthur New Testament Commentary*, 1–3 John, 129–130.

35   Richards, *The Teacher's Commentary*, 1 John 4:12–13.

36   David Jeremiah, *What Are You Afraid Of? Facing Down Your Fears with Faith* (Carol Stream, IL: Tyndale, 2013), introduction.

37   Wiersbe, *The Bible Exposition Commentary*, Romans 14:10–12.

38   www.biblestudytools.com/lexicons/greek/nas/nike.html.

39   MacArthur, *MacArthur New Testament Commentary*, 1–3 John, 184–186.

40   Max Lucado, *Before Amen* (Nashville: Thomas Nelson, 2014), 6–7.

41   Ibid.

42   John D. Grassmick, in *The Bible Knowledge Commentary*, Mark 3:28–30.

43   Ibid.

44   Warren W. Wiersbe, *Be Real: Turning from Hypocrisy to Truth*, Commentary on 1 John (Colorado Springs: David C. Cook, 1972).

45   *Strong's Greek Dictionary of the New Testament*, #680.

46   MacArthur, *MacArthur New Testament Commentary*, 1–3 John, 210.

Proverbs 31 Ministries

If you were inspired by Wendy Blight or *I Am Loved* and desire to deepen your own personal relationship with Jesus Christ, we encourage you to connect with Proverbs 31 Ministries.

Proverbs 31 Ministries exists to be a trusted friend who will take you by the hand and walk by your side, leading you one step closer to the heart of God through:

- ♥ Free online daily devotions
- ♥ First 5 Bible study app
- ♥ Daily radio program
- ♥ Books and resources
- ♥ Online Bible Studies
- ♥ COMPEL Writers Training: www.CompelTraining.com
- ♥ Speakers for events

To learn more about Proverbs 31 Ministries, call 877-731-4663 or visit www.Proverbs31.org.

Proverbs 31 Ministries
630 Team Rd., Suite 100
Matthews, NC 28105
www.Proverbs31.org

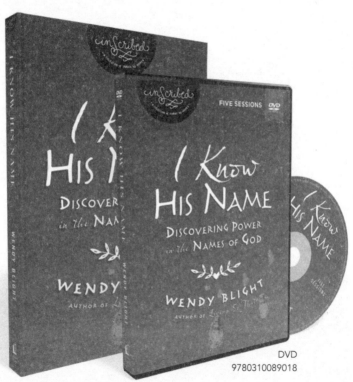

Stop Walking in Circles

We all carry habits and hang-ups that can sometimes stop us from getting that promotion, hurt our relationships with those closest to us, or stunt our growth toward deeper levels of intimacy. You know who God is calling you to be, but sometimes wonder how you're ever going to get there. This journey through Exodus is designed to give you tools to help you break those bad habits and move you into your promised land: that place God is calling you to.

Women will learn more about one of the most important parts of God's story—the exodus of His children out of captivity with the world ahead of them. What stopped them? It will leave readers leaning in, asking what is stopping me?

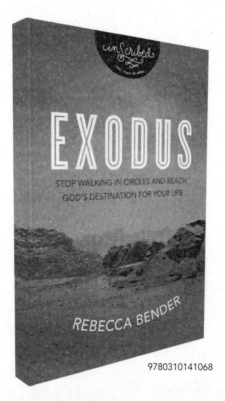

9780310141068

— AVAILABLE NOVEMBER 2021 —

HarperChristian Resources

Every woman's reference for how to live in bold confidence.

Have you ever needed confidence in a specific circumstance and couldn't think of an example of anyone who had "been there, overcome that"?

Author and Speaker Lynn Cowell took every form of insecurity we experience as women and asked God to reveal how we should respond. The result is this in-depth 6-session video Bible study spanning obscure and house-hold name stories of women in Scripture who demonstrate unshakable confidence no matter their circumstances.

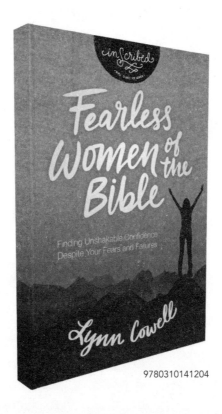

9780310141204

— AVAILABLE JANUARY 2022 —

HarperChristian Resources

Discover the Beauty of God's Word

The Beautiful Word™ Bible Study Series helps you connect God's Word to your daily life through vibrant video teaching, group discussion, and deep personal study that includes verse-by-verse reading, Scripture memory, coloring pages, and encouragement to receive your own beautiful Word from God.

In each study, a central theme—a beautiful word—threads throughout the book, helping you connect and apply each book of the Bible to your daily life today, and forever.

IN THIS SERIES:

GALATIANS — Jada Edwards — Available Now
REVELATION — Margaret Feinberg — Available Now
EPHESIANS — Lori Wilhite — Available Now
ROMANS — Jada Edwards — December 2021